Comida Sabrosa

COMIDA SABROSA

Home-Style Southwestern Cooking

Irene Barraza Sanchez
and Gloria Sanchez Yund

Illustrations by Cyd Riley

University of New Mexico Press • Albuquerque

Design by Barbara Jellow

First spiralbound printing, 2001

Library of Congress Cataloging-in-Publication Data

Sanchez, Irene Barraza, 1948–
    Comida sabrosa: home-style Southwestern cooking.
    Includes index.
       1. Cookery, American—New Mexico.
2. Cookery, American—Colorado.
3. Cookery (Hot peppers).
I. Yund, Gloria Sanchez, 1949–
II. Title.
TX715.S1962 1982   641.59789   82-10904
ISBN 0-8263-2386-3

To our mothers,
Trini Chavez Sanchez and
Isabel Paiz Barraza, to
whose expertise we attribute
our skills in cooking

Contents

The authors of *Comida Sabrosa* are sisters-in-law. Irene Barraza Sanchez grew up in Gallup, New Mexico. Her mother taught her to cook, and she enjoys experimenting with native foods and spices, taking particular pride in her baking. A legal secretary, Irene lives with her husband in the solar-heated house they designed and built for themselves in Tomé, New Mexico, an old farming community south of Albuquerque in the Rio Grande Valley.

Gloria Sanchez Yund was born and raised in Albuquerque. A graduate of New Mexico State University with a B.S. degree in home economics, she has taught home economics in the public schools in New Mexico and Colorado. Several of her recipes have taken awards in chile shows in both states. Gloria lives in Del Norte, Colorado, with her husband and five children. Currently she teaches Southwestern cooking at the community school near her home.

We compiled this cookbook in an effort to preserve our beautiful culture and heritage. But we have also tried to make it easy to read and easy for everyone to use—to learn to cook these dishes, to become a better cook, or to plan a party.

We have tested and tasted each recipe. Many of them have been used in classes on Southwest-style cooking, and we know that they are practical, versatile, and economical.

We have dedicated this book to our mothers, but we owe debts of gratitude to other members of our families. We are especially grateful to our fathers, the late Carlos Sanchez, whose love for gardening produced some of the finest chile in the Southwest, and Adolph Barraza, whose appreciation for the finest chile made us more aware of the incomparable foods of our culture.

To our patient and understanding husbands, Charlie and Ted, we are also grateful, especially for their beneficial advice and enduring encouragement.

Introduction

What is Southwest-style cooking? One of North America's oldest cuisines, it is also one of the most popular contemporary regional styles of cooking. The Southwestern cuisine that produced the recipes in this book is basically New Mexican and southern Coloradan. It is not Texan, or Mexican, or Californian, although some dishes and ingredients that appear in this book also turn up in those regions. Many of the dishes and ingredients that characterize Southwest-style cooking have been in use in the New World since pre-Columbian times. The Indian, Spanish, Mexican, and European cultures have all contributed ingredients and techniques.

Although we have compiled these recipes in an effort to preserve the New Mexican culture that has been handed down to us from generations past, we want them to be easy to use. From wood stove to microwave, many of our recipes have been adapted for today's life-styles and equipment. Beans, tortillas, and chile sauces are the basic ingredients used to produce New Mexican dishes. In this book we have gone beyond the basics to attract both the novice cook and the connoisseur. We have also included some Hispanic recipes that are not strictly Southwestern, for just as modern cooks are able to take advantage of such tools as the microwave and the food processor, our repertoires are all broadened by modern supermarkets, where we can buy jalapeños almost all year round in many parts of the country.

Whether you want to start from scratch, roasting your own fresh chiles and making your own tortillas, or take advantage of the Southwestern foods available in cans and mixes at your supermarket, we wish you good eating with our families' favorite recipes for *comida sabrosa—* tasty food!

Availability of Southwestern Foods

CHILE

The most distinctive ingredient in Southwest cuisine is chile, and we give you more information on chile on pages 37–49. New Mexico's pungent chiles have a widespread reputation. Fresh New Mexico chiles are incomparable. A native New Mexican would not dream of using anything else, and many people drive miles to obtain fresh green or red chiles. In some parts of the country, unfortunately, fresh chile is not available. It is important, therefore, for the consumer to become familiar with what is available in his or her area.

Frozen green chile is probably the next best thing to the fresh variety. Frozen green chiles are already peeled and roasted, so they are ready for immediate use.

If frozen chiles are not available in your area, you are almost sure to be able to buy *canned green chile*, usually grown in New Mexico. This product is popular because of its convenience and long shelf life. You can buy canned chiles either whole or chopped.

Dry red chile pods are becoming more readily available in supermarkets in the Southwest, probably because enchiladas are so popular.

In Southwestern markets *powdered red chile* is also available. This is not to be confused with the powder packaged by large spice companies and labeled *chile powder*. Chile powder is a blend of powdered chiles, cumin, and other spices.

Jalapeños are generally found pickled, in cans. They are most often used in garnishes. In season, many western markets carry fresh jalapeños.

The *pequín* used in hot sauces is an extremely pungent pepper. It is found as a whole pod or crushed and ready for use in sauce, in the seasoning section of a supermarket or in a gourmet shop.

Increasingly available are a variety of prepared chile *sauces* and *salsas*. Generally these are clearly labeled with suggestions for use. Shopping around and sampling different brands and varieties is an enjoyable way to find out which kind of salsa you like on your eggs, tacos, hamburgers, pizza, or almost anything else—this seasoning is addictive! We have included several recipes for chile sauces in our Chile section.

BREADS

Flour tortillas, once available only if you made them at home, are now available in western supermarkets in the dairy section. You can buy either thick, home-style tortillas, or very thin ones. They also come in large and small diameters.

Corn tortillas can be made at home, but today most cooks use store-bought ones. In the West they are available fresh at your supermarket. Elsewhere you will probably be able to buy them in cans.

Sopaipillas, a New Mexican fried bread, can be bought frozen in some markets. A mix is available in many markets throughout the country.

BEANS

Pinto beans are the variety most often used in Southwest-style cooking. If you can't buy them in the produce department, where you can scoop them out of a bin, you will find them packaged along with the other dried beans.

Pinto beans are also available in cans, either whole or refried.

If you cannot find pinto beans in your part of the country, substitute kidney beans.

More information about all these ingredients, and others, is available in the Glossary.

Glossary

Albondigas: Meatballs; sometimes served as appetizers

Aperitivo: Appetizer

Arroz: Rice

Arroz con pollo: Chicken with rice

Arroz dulce: Rice pudding. Literally, sweet rice.

Atole: A blue cornmeal gruel, served as a beverage with sugar or as a hot cereal with milk and sugar

Biscochitos: Anise-flavored rolled cookies, traditionally shaped like fleur de lys and sprinkled with cinnamon and sugar

Blue cornmeal: Cornmeal ground from dark blue corn

Buñuelo: Fried puff pastry resembling a sopaipilla, served with a glaze or dipped in cinnamon and sugar

Burrito: Flour tortilla filled with beans or meat and served with a salsa and garnished with lettuce, tomato, and onion

Calabaza: Squash, pumpkin, and related vegetables

Capirotada: Sweet bread pudding with cinnamon, raisins, nuts, and cheese

Carne: Meat

Carne adovada: Pork marinated in red chile sauce

Carne asada: Brazier-cooked meat

Carne molida: Ground beef

Chalupa: Boat-shaped fried corn tortilla filled with beans, cheese, lettuce

Chicos: Dried sweet corn kernels

Chile caribe: Red chile pods ground and blended with water

Chile colorado: Red chile

Chile con queso: Chile with cheese; usually served as a dip with tostados

Chile pequín: Thin, very hot red chiles about 1½ inches long

Chile powder: A commercially mixed blend of powdered red chile and other ingredients such as cumin and coriander

Chile relleno: Green chile stuffed with cheese, dipped in egg batter, and fried. Literally, stuffed chile.

Chile verde: Green chile

Chimichanga: Fried burrito topped with salsa and/or sour cream

Chicharrones: Cracklings made from pork fat with about ¼ inch of meat

Chorizo: Highly seasoned Mexican pork sausage

Chuleta: Pork chop with red chile sauce

Corn tortilla: Flat bread cooked on a griddle. Can be made from either yellow or blue corn. Most cooks use store-bought corn tortillas. *See also flour tortilla.*

Enchiladas: Corn tortillas served rolled or flat filled with ground beef and/or cheese, onions, and chile. A variety of toppings or sauces may accompany enchiladas

Flan: A baked custard with caramel sauce

Flauta: Fried version of a taco, rolled thin, often dipped in sour cream or guacamole. Literally, flute.

Flour tortilla: Flat bread cooked on a griddle, made with flour. *See also corn tortilla.*

Frijoles: Beans

Gorditas: Masa stuffed with seasoned meat and fried

Guacamole: Avocado dip

Harina: Flour

Horno: Outdoor oven, usually made of adobe and beehive shaped

Huevos rancheros: Literally, ranch-style eggs, served with corn tortillas and salsa

Leche: Milk

Masa: Dough made of dried, ground corn and lime water

Masa harina: A dried mix to which water is added to make dough

Menudo: In New Mexico, pork skins used in posole. Elsewhere, *menudo* is a tripe stew.

Mollete: Anise bread

Nachos: Tostados topped with cheese and green chile and baked; served as appetizers or with drinks

Natilla: Pudding sprinkled with cinnamon and nutmeg

Pastelitos: "Little pies" that are served in square portions

Pollo: Chicken

Posole: Hominy; corn kernels treated with lime

Quelitas: Spinach mixed with pinto beans, bacon, and crushed red chile pods

Queso: Cheese

Ristra: A string of chiles

Refrito: Refried; usually describes beans that are cooked, mashed, and "refried"

Salsa: Hot sauce usually made with fresh chile, tomatoes, and onions

Salsa pequín: A very hot salsa made with chile pequín, often labeled *taco sauce*

Salsa rancherita: A very thick salsa made with onions, green chile, tomatoes, and seasonings

Sopa: Sweet bread pudding with raisins, cinnamon, nuts, cheese

Sopaipilla: Fried bread, made with either yeast or baking powder

Sopaipilla compuesta: An open-faced "stuffed" sopaipilla made with refried beans, green chile, cheese, lettuce

Tamale: Masa filled with pork and red chile, cooked by steaming in a corn husk

Taco: A corn tortilla filled with meat or beans and topped with cheese, lettuce, tomatoes, onions, and salsa pequín

Torta: Stiffly beaten egg, fried and served with red chile

Tortilla: See corn tortilla and flour tortilla.

Tostada: Open-faced taco

Tostados: Corn tortillas cut into wedges, fried until crisp, sprinkled with salt

APPETIZERS

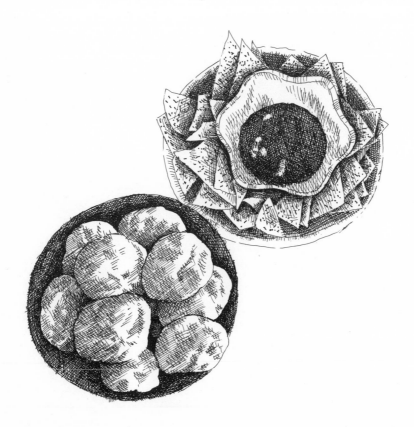

Chile con Queso Dip

Cheese and chile lovers, you'll enjoy this one!

1 large onion, chopped
½ cup butter
1 16 oz. can tomatoes, well drained, chopped
1 cup chopped, roasted green chile, or ½ cup chopped jalapeños
2 lbs. Velveeta cheese, cubed
1 teaspoon garlic salt
1 teaspoon onion salt

SAUTE onion in butter.
ADD tomatoes (chopped) and green chile.
SIMMER slowly until most of liquid is evaporated.
ADD cubed cheese a little at a time. (Be careful not to burn cheese. Keep burner on very low heat.) Add salts.
KEEP warm. (A fondue pot is useful for this step.)
SERVE with homemade tostado chips.
MAKES 3–4 cups.

Chile con Queso Puffs

These appetizers taste like chile rellenos; the shells can be made in advance and frozen until ready for use.

1 cup water
½ cup butter or margarine
¼ teaspoon salt
1 cup flour
4 eggs

GREASE large cookie sheet.
HEAT water, butter or margarine, and salt in 3-quart saucepan over medium heat until butter melts and mixture boils. Remove from heat.
ADD flour all at once.
STIR vigorously until mixture forms a ball.
ADD eggs, one at a time.
BEAT well after each egg.
DROP batter by quarter-cups on greased cookie sheet, in mounds 3 inches apart; swirl tops of each.
BAKE 30 minutes at 425° or until golden brown. Remove cookie sheet from oven.
SLIT sides of each puff to let steam escape.
REPLACE in oven and bake 10 minutes longer.

COOL puffs on wire rack.
SLICE puffs and fill with chile con queso (page 10).
SERVE warm or cold.
MAKES 2–3 dozen, depending on size.

Option: ¼ lb. browned ground beef or venison may be added to chile con queso and spooned into puff shells.

Salsa Pequín Sour Cream Dip

Try this zesty dip with your favorite crisp vegetables.

1 cup prepared salsa pequín (page 43) 1 pint sour cream	MIX together sauce and sour cream. SERVE with any of the following: fresh cauliflower buds, carrot sticks, celery sticks, jicama slices OR potato or taco chips.

Chicharrones
FRIED PORK SKINS

A crunchy treat with beer!

2 lbs. raw pork fat and skins salt	DICE pork fat with skins into 2-inch squares. COOK pork fat and skins over medium heat in large cast-iron skillet until brown and crisp. REMOVE from skillet and drain on paper towel. Add salt to taste. SERVE either hot or cold. MAKES 4–6 ½ cup servings.

Nachos

Try these munchies at your next cocktail party!

1 package of 12 corn tortillas
oil
longhorn cheese, sliced
½ cup chopped green chile
garlic salt

CUT each tortilla into 8 pie-shaped wedges.
FRY in oil over medium heat until crisp.
DRAIN on absorbent towel.
PLACE slice of cheese on each tortilla wedge. Top with a piece of green chile. Sprinkle with garlic salt.
BROIL until cheese melts.
SERVE immediately.
MAKES 8 dozen.

Queso con Miel

CHEESE WITH HONEY

Our parents and grandparents ate this nutritious snack often.

1 lb. longhorn cheese
honey, sugar, or syrup

SLICE cheese ¼–½ inch thick.
DIP each slice in honey, sugar, or syrup.

Chile Cheese Pinwheels

1 cup chopped green chile
3 oz. softened cream cheese
1½ cups grated cheddar or longhorn
   cheese
½ teaspoon onion salt or 1 small
   onion, chopped
¼ teaspoon garlic salt
1 pkg. (8 count) crescent roll
   refrigerator dough

MIX chile, cheeses, onion salt or
   onion, and garlic salt until smooth.
ROLL and press 2 crescent triangles to
   form a rectangle; spread evenly
   with creamed mixture.
ROLL jelly-roll fashion, pressing
   seams together.
REPEAT with remaining ingredients.
SLICE ¼ inch thick.
BAKE at 375° 10–15 minutes or until
   lightly browned.
SERVE warm.
MAKES 1½–2 dozen.

Tostados

*Served warm and sprinkled with a little salt, these homemade chips
are better than store-bought.*

1 package (12 count) corn tortillas
salt
oil

HEAT oil in cast-iron skillet over
   medium heat.
CUT tortillas into 8 pie-shaped wedges.
FRY tortillas until crisp.
DRAIN on paper towel.
SPRINKLE with salt.
SERVE with your favorite dip.
MAKES about 8 dozen.

Chile-Stuffed Puffs

These are appetizer-size compuestas.

1 recipe sopaipillas (page 30)
1 recipe refried beans (page 105)
½ cup chopped green chile
½ cup grated longhorn cheese
1 medium tomato, diced
½ cup chopped onion

PREPARE sopaipillas as directed,
  only make each sopaipilla a 2-inch
  square.
AFTER frying each sopaipilla, cool on
  wire rack; slit each along one side.
STUFF each sopaipilla with refried
  beans.
SPRINKLE top of sopaipilla with
  chile, cheese, tomato, and onion.
SERVE immediately.
MAKES 4–5 dozen.

Fruit Appetizers

*Fresh fruits in season will make these kabobs a colorful addition to
any buffet table.*

pineapple chunks (1 20-oz. can) or
  other fruit in bite-size pieces
1 pint sour cream
2 cups shredded coconut
2 cups maraschino cherries (1
  medium-size jar)

DIP pineapple chunks in sour cream
  and roll in coconut.
ARRANGE fruit, alternating pineapple
  chunks and cherries for color effect
  on toothpicks or mini skewers.

Guacamole

AVOCADO DIP

For an even creamier dip, substitute sour cream for mayonnaise.

2–3 large very ripe avocados
¼–½ cup mayonnaise
1 teaspoon dry onion or
1 tablespoon fresh chopped onion
¼ teaspoon garlic salt
¼ cup green chile, finely chopped

MIX all ingredients in a blender or food processor until creamy.
COVER with plastic wrap until ready to serve. This prevents darkening or drying.
REFRIGERATE until serving time.
SERVE with chips or homemade tostados.
MAKES 2 cups.

Chile Verde Masa Albondigas

GREEN CHILE DOUGHBALLS

2 cups Bisquick
½ cup chopped green chile
1 lb. pork sausage, uncooked
2 cups grated cheddar cheese
1 teaspoon onion salt
1 teaspoon garlic salt

MIX all ingredients together well.
ROLL mixture into 1-inch balls.
PLACE on a greased cookie sheet.
BAKE at 425° for 35 minutes.
MAKES 2 dozen.

Chile Tortilla Appetizers

1 recipe flour tortillas (page 28)
8 oz. softened cream cheese
1 cup chopped green chile
1 tablespoon minced onion
½ teaspoon garlic salt

PREPARE tortilla dough as directed, but roll very thin; cut with 2″ or 3″ round cookie cutter; cook on heavy cast-iron skillet until lightly browned. Cool.

CREAM cheese, green chile, and onion; add garlic salt.

SPREAD creamed mixture over each mini tortilla; garnish with an olive slice, if desired.

MAKES 2–3 dozen.

Option: Prepare tortilla dough as directed, but roll to rectangular size. Cook and cool. Spread creamed mixture over each rectangle, and layer creamed mixture and tortilla alternately in stacks of five. Cut into 2- or 3-inch squares and place toothpick through center of each.

MAKES 1½–2 dozen appetizers.

Chile and Frijole Dip

This dip can be used as a taco spread also. Cut fried corn tortillas in half, fill each half with 1 tablespoon dip, roll and hold together with colored toothpicks, and serve as a mini taco.

1 lb. ground beef
½ cup chopped onion
1 teaspoon garlic salt
1 teaspoon salt
1 tablespoon red powder chile
2 cups refried beans (page 105)
¼ cup water
½ cup grated longhorn cheese

BROWN ground beef in skillet with onion.
DRAIN excess fat.
ADD salts, chile powder, beans, and water.
HEAT, stirring constantly.
PLACE in fondue dish and serve warm with tostados.
IF DESIRED, sprinkle grated cheese over top of dip at serving time.
MAKES about 1 quart.

BEVERAGES

Cinnamon Coffee

6 cups water
3 sticks cinnamon
3 tablespoons ground coffee
(not instant)

POUR water into large saucepan or
stove-top coffee pot. Add cinnamon
sticks.
BRING to a boil.
ADD ground coffee and boil only until
water becomes a medium brown;
the darker brown, the stronger the
coffee.
SERVE hot with sugar and cream or
1 tablespoon whipped cream
per cup.
MAKES 6 servings.

Café con Leche
COFFEE WITH MILK

*This beverage brings back fond memories of Papa Ramón and his
wood stove.*

1 pot of strong coffee
milk, scalded

PREPARE strong coffee.
SERVE in individual cups ¼ cup full
only.
ADD ¾ cup hot milk to each cup.
SERVE immediately.
MAKES 4–6 cups.

New Mexican Hot Chocolate

Excellent with buñuelos (page 116).

½ cup sugar
¼ cup cocoa
1½ cups cold water
1 teaspoon cinnamon
½ teaspoon nutmeg
6 cups milk
1 tablespoon vanilla
whipped cream for topping

COMBINE sugar, cocoa, water, and spices; cook over medium heat; add milk and scald.
STIR until smooth.
ADD vanilla and top with whipped cream.
SPRINKLE with dash nutmeg and cinnamon or serve with a whole cinnamon stick.
MAKES 6 servings.

Option: If Mexican chocolate is available, substitute 2 sections Mexican chocolate for cocoa. (Mexican chocolate actually comes in round sections, not squares.)

Atolé

This gruel was once used for medicinal purposes, to soothe an upset stomach or diarrhea.

1 cup blue cornmeal
1 cup cold water
2 cups boiling water
milk
sugar

MIX cornmeal and cold water.
ADD cornmeal to boiling water and
    boil until mixture thickens.
SIMMER 5 minutes.
SERVE hot with milk and sugar.
MAKES 2 cups.

Manzanilla Tea

CHAMOMILE TEA

Manzanilla tea is wonderfully soothing. Mama gave this tea to her children when they were colicky or simply to warm them before bedtime.

2 cups water
2 tablespoons dried chamomile
4 teaspoons sugar

HEAT water to boiling.
ADD chamomile.
BOIL till water looks lightly tea-
    colored; pour through strainer or
    cheesecloth.
ADD sugar and serve as a tea.
MAKES 2 cups.

NOTE: this tea may be served hot or cold, but is traditionally served hot.

Rompopé

EGGNOG

The traditional Christmas drink; also rich and nourishing.

6 eggs, separated
1 quart half and half
½ cup sugar
1 tablespoon vanilla
nutmeg

BEAT egg yolks well; add half and half and sugar. Set aside.
BEAT egg whites until stiff and fold gently into egg yolk mixture.
ADD vanilla and chill.
WHEN ready to serve, sprinkle dash of nutmeg over each serving.
MAKES 1 quart.

Option: Add 1 jigger (1½ oz.) bourbon for each serving.

Sangria de Ramón

1 cup sugar
1 cup water
1 lime
1 lemon
1 orange
1 quart red wine
1 quart club soda
ice cubes

MIX sugar and water to form syrup.
    Set aside.
MIX syrup with wine and club soda.
POUR into chilled glasses.
GARNISH with lime, lemon, and
    orange slices.
MAKES 4–6 wine glasses.

New Mexico Screwdriver

A close relative of the tequila sunrise.

2 oz. tequila
1 tablespoon lime juice
1 tablespoon grenadine
½ cup strained orange juice
crushed ice
1 lime, sliced

PLACE all ingredients in blender and
    blend until smooth.
SERVE chilled in 8 oz. glasses,
    garnished with slices of lime.
MAKES 2–3 drinks.

Piña Colada

2 6 oz. cans pineapple juice
1 tablespoon powdered sugar
½ cup coconut juice or prepared piña
    colada mixer
2 oz. dark rum
crushed ice

PLACE all ingredients except rum and
    ice in blender.
BLEND until smooth.
ADD ice and rum and blend until just
    smooth.
SERVE immediately in 8 oz. glasses.
MAKES 3–4 drinks.

Option: For a more tangy flavor, add 1
small can (drained) crushed pineapple
before blending.
GARNISH with pineapple wedge and
maraschino cherry.

Margaritas

Licking the salt from the rim of the glass is half the fun of this drink. Special margarita glasses with hollow stems are fun, but you can enjoy margaritas out of any glasses.

6 oz. tequila
¾ cup fresh lime juice
6 oz. triple sec
crushed ice
salt

PLACE all ingredients, except salt, in blender and blend until smooth; chill glasses.
WHEN ready to serve, wet glass rim, dip in salt, and pour chilled mixture into glass.
MAKES 2–3 drinks.

BREADS

Flour Tortillas

Tortillas are wonderful eaten with butter while still hot.

2 cups flour
1 teaspoon salt
1 teaspoon baking powder
2 tablespoons shortening (use bacon drippings, if desired)
¼–½ cup very warm water

COMBINE flour, salt, and baking powder in large bowl.

CUT in shortening; add water and mix well until dough is solid, adding more water or flour as necessary. Dough should be pliable.

COVER bowl with dishtowel, and let dough rest about 5 minutes.

HEAT heavy cast-iron griddle or skillet.

SEPARATE dough into fist-size balls; pat each ball into 5-inch pattie; roll into circle with rolling pin from center of dough outward until dough is ¼–½ inch thick and 7–8 inches in diameter.

COOK on skillet until blistered; flip on
 other side.
COOL tortillas on plate covered with
 paper towel or dish towel to
 prevent sticking and sogginess. Do
 not stack tortillas until they
 are cool.
SERVE in place of bread with any
 meal.
STORE in plastic bag.
TORTILLAS freeze well. They will
 keep several weeks.
MAKES 6–8.

Option: 1 cup whole wheat flour and
1 cup enriched flour may be used in
place of 2 cups flour.

Yeast Sopaipillas

Sopaipillas, a fried bread, are eaten with honey. They can also be stuffed with beans and meat.

4 cups flour
1½ teaspoons salt
1 tablespoon sugar
1 teaspoon baking powder
1 tablespoon shortening
1 pkg. dry yeast
¼ cup warm water (110°)
1¼ cup scalded milk, cooled
oil for frying

PLACE dry ingredients in large bowl; cut in shortening; set aside.
DISSOLVE yeast in warm water; add sugar and stir well.
MAKE a well in center of dry ingredients; add liquid ingredients all at once.
MIX to form a workable dough.
KNEAD dough for 5–10 minutes. Set aside.
COVER dough with towel and let dough rest for 15 minutes.
HEAT oil in deep skillet (420°).
ROLL dough ⅛ inch thick into rectangle; cut into 4″ squares, or rectangles.
DEEP fry each square until golden brown on both sides; drain on absorbent towel.
SERVE warm with honey.
MAKES 3–4 dozen.

Option: For baking powder sopaipillas, increase baking powder to 3 teaspoons and omit dry yeast.

Navajo Fry Bread

Navajos take credit for this bread. This particular version resembles the popular sopaipilla except that it is 4–5 inches in diameter and has a hole in the center.

2 cups flour
4 teaspoons baking powder
1 teaspoon salt
2 tablespoons shortening
⅔ cup warm water
oil for frying

COMBINE dry ingredients. Cut in shortening.
ADD water to make a workable dough; tear off dough into fist-size balls.
ROLL dough ½ inch thick to form a circle; with finger, make a hole in the center of the dough (about the size of a dime).
DEEP fry in hot oil until golden brown; drain on absorbent towel.
SERVE hot with honey.
MAKES 1–2 dozen.

NOTE: Traditionally, Navajo cooks do not roll out the dough. They flip it back and forth between their hands until it expands into a circle.

Mama Libby's Hot Rolls

*Mama baked these in a wood stove and they disappeared quickly as
they came out hot and golden brown.*

5 cups flour
½ cup powdered milk
¼ cup sugar
1 teaspoon salt
½ cup shortening
1½ cups warm water
2 pkgs. dry yeast

PLACE 3–4 cups flour in large bowl;
add powdered milk, sugar, and salt.
CUT in shortening.
HEAT water until hot, but not boiling;
stir in dry yeast. Add liquid to flour
mixture and blend until smooth.
Add enough flour to make a
smooth, solid dough. Knead 5–10
minutes.
PLACE dough in well-greased bowl;
cover and let rise 1 hour in warm
place.
PUNCH dough down; break dough
into fist-size pieces; grease two 8- or
9-inch round pans; round off each
piece of dough to form a bun
shape.
PLACE in greased pans; cover and let
rise 1 hour.
BAKE at 375° 25–30 minutes or until
golden brown.
MAKES 1–1½ dozen.

Indian Bread

A unique sourdoughlike bread often baked outdoors in an horno.

2 tablespoons shortening or lard
1 teaspoon sugar or 1 tablespoon
  honey
1 teaspoon salt
5 cups flour
1 cup warm water
1 pkg. dry yeast

PLACE 3 cups flour, sugar, and salt in large bowl; cut in shortening; make well in center.

HEAT water to warm, but not hot, stir in yeast, and mix well. If using honey instead of sugar, add to liquid.

ADD liquid to dry ingredients; mix well, adding flour until a solid dough is formed. Knead 5 minutes.

GREASE sides of bowl and let rise in warm place 1 hour. Punch down and knead dough again.

GREASE a 2-quart round baking dish; shape dough into a circular mound; place in dish to rise 45 minutes.

BAKE at 375° for about 50 minutes or until bread is lightly browned and sounds hollow when thumped lightly.

MAKES 1 large loaf.

Chile con Queso Bread

This bread is an excellent accompaniment to any meat dish.

1 loaf French bread
¼ cup chopped green chile
4 tablespoons mayonnaise
½ teaspoon onion salt
½ teaspoon garlic salt
⅔ cup grated cheddar or longhorn
   cheese

MIX chile, mayonnaise, salts, and
   cheese.
SLICE bread into 12 slices; cut each
   slice in half.
BAKE sliced bread on 2 cookie sheets at
   425° 4 minutes or until lightly
   browned.
REMOVE cookie sheets from oven;
   turn bread untoasted side up;
   spread 1–2 tablespoons cheese
   mixture on untoasted side of each
   slice.
BROIL 3 minutes or until cheese is
   melted and bubbly.
SERVE immediately.
MAKES 24 pieces.

Cornbread

This is a very light cornbread. Serve it with your next pot of beans.

1 cup flour
1 cup cornmeal
1 tablespoon baking powder
1 teaspoon salt
¼ cup sugar, if desired
2 eggs
1 cup milk
¼ cup shortening or oil

MIX dry ingredients.
ADD eggs, milk, and shortening.
BEAT just until smooth; do not overbeat.
POUR into greased 8-inch round or square pan or cornbread skillet.
BAKE at 425° for 35–40 minutes or until golden brown.
MAKES 4–6 servings.

Options: For green chile cornbread, add ¼ cup chopped green chile and omit sugar. For blue corn bread, substitute blue cornmeal for yellow cornmeal.

CHILE and
CHILE SAUCES

Chile (also spelled *chili*) is a term with several meanings. In this book the word *chile* designates not the dish that is a mixture of beans, meat, and chile seasoning, but rather the pungent capsicum pepper pod. Red chile is the mature version of green chile.

All chile derives its distinctive flavor and pungency from the chemical compound capsaicin, which is concentrated mainly around the stem. The pungency of any chile depends not only on what variety of the capsicum family the chile belongs to but also on the growing conditions.

The flavor and pungency of chile range from mild to almost sweet to painfully hot. Although experts can identify the hotter chiles by their shape, it is more reliable to purchase peppers labeled *hot*, *medium*, or *mild*.

Chile is a rich source of vitamins A and C. The amount of both these vitamins increases as the chile matures. They reach their maximum level at harvest time.

Dried chile loses vitamin C because of the effects of heat and oxidation. Red chile, however, acts as a preservative in, for example, frozen dishes made with red chile sauce.

Chile Preparation

The acid in chile often irritates the skin, especially when you are peeling green chile. To avoid being burned, use either of the following methods as a preventative measure:

1. Wear rubber gloves, or
2. rub hands with shortening to form a protective seal over the skin. *Do this before you peel chile.*

To soothe the tingling burns that can result if you don't protect your hands, soak your hands in milk. If your hands

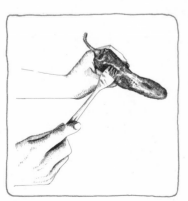

are exposed to the juice of the chile, *do not rub your eyes.* If chile does come in contact with eyes or mucous membranes, flush immediately with cold water.

Green Chile

ROASTING GREEN CHILE

PURCHASE: one bushel fresh green chile, which will result in approximately 18 to 20 half-pint sacks for freezing.

SELECT: fresh chiles that are firm, smooth-textured, thick fleshed, shiny, and have a fresh pungent odor.

WASH: pods and dry with absorbent towels.

PIERCE: chiles with fork tines to keep chile from bursting while roasting.

PLACE: chile on any of the following: cookie sheets for oven broiler units (place 3–4 inches away from broiler unit), or cast-iron skillet or griddle (for stove-top roasting), or charcoal grill.

ROAST: by blistering evenly on all sides.

COOL: by placing chiles in a pan, sprinkling with small amount of water, and covering with a damp towel. Leave towel on chiles until completely cool and ready to peel.

PEEL: holding chile from stem and peeling blistered skins downward. After skin is peeled, remove stem and seeds.

Methods of Preserving Green Chile

Freezing with skin attached

COOL: chile after roasting.

PACKAGE: in freezer-weight containers (½ pint and pint are most commonly used sizes).

DEFROST: when ready to use. Peel when thawed.

USE: in any green chile recipe (whole pods are very good for use in chile rellenos).

Freezing with skin removed

COOL: chile after roasting.

REMOVE: outer skin, seeds, and stem.

CHOP: very fine.

PACKAGE: in freezer-weight containers (half-pint and pint are most commonly used sizes).

DEFROST: when ready to use.

USE: in any of your favorite green chile recipes with the exception of those calling for use of whole chile.

Drying

YOU WILL NEED: roasted, cooled, and peeled green chiles (do not remove pod or stem), string or twine, cheesecloth.

TIE: together in clusters of 3 chiles. Tie several clusters of chiles on same string to form a continuous row. End result will resemble a small ristra.

HANG: ristra outdoors, covering chiles with cheesecloth to protect from insects and rodents.

DRY: chiles completely.

USE: in recipes calling for green chile.

Salsa Verde con Carne

GREEN CHILE SAUCE WITH MEAT

Que salsa tan sabrosa . . . (What a tasty sauce!) A zesty condiment over a basic burrito or a hot bowl of pinto beans.

1 lb. lean ground beef or cubed pork
½ cup chopped green chile
¼ teaspoon onion salt
¼ teaspoon garlic salt
¼ cup flour or cornstarch
1¼ cups water

BROWN meat; remove excess fat.
ADD chopped chile and salts.
PREPARE a gravy paste by mixing flour and ¼ cup water; pour in 1 cup water and add to meat mixture; stir well.
SIMMER 10–15 minutes.
MAKES 1 quart.

Chile Verde

This finely chopped chile can be used in salsas, relishes, or as a sandwich spread instead of mustard.

½ pint fresh roasted or frozen green chile
2 small cloves garlic, minced
¼ teaspoon salt

PEEL skin from green chile.
REMOVE seeds and stems.
CHOP chile very fine; add minced garlic and salt.
MIX well.
STORE in refrigerator 1–2 weeks and use as needed.
MAKES 1 cup.

Nana's Green Chile Sauce

1 lb. ground beef
2 tablespoons bacon drippings or oil
4 tablespoons flour or cornstarch
1 cup water
1 cup chopped green chile
2 stewed tomatoes, peeled and diced
2 potatoes, peeled, boiled, and diced
1 teaspoon onion salt or 1 tablespoon
 minced onion
1 teaspoon garlic salt or 1 small clove
 garlic, minced

BROWN ground beef in large skillet;
 drain excess fat; set beef aside.
HEAT bacon drippings or oil in same
 skillet.
ADD flour or cornstarch and stir until
 lightly browned.
ADD water and stir to form gravy.
ADD beef, chile, tomatoes, potatoes,
 onion, and garlic.
SIMMER until gravy thickens; if gravy
 becomes too thick, add ¼–½
 cup water.
SERVE immediately.
MAKES 1½–2 cups.

Salsa Pequín

*This sauce is not only an excellent dip to serve with tostados, but
also good poured over huevos rancheros or as a sauce for a taco dish.*

1 12 oz. can tomato juice or tomato
    sauce
2 tablespoons minced dry onion
1 tablespoon chile pequín
1 tablespoon garlic powder
1 tablespoon sugar
1 teaspoon cumin
1 teaspoon black pepper
1 teaspoon whole ground oregano
1 teaspoon seasoning salt, optional
¼ cup chopped green chile

PLACE all ingredients in a stainless
    steel saucepan.
SIMMER over low heat for 1 hour.
MAKES about 3 cups.

Salsa Rancherita

This succulent sauce compliments egg or burrito dishes.

2 tablespoons minced onion
3 tablespoons butter
4 fresh tomatoes
1 cup chopped green chile
2 cloves garlic, chopped
1 tablespoon oregano
1 teaspoon salt
¼ teaspoon pepper

SAUTE onions in butter until they are transparent.
ADD tomatoes, chile, garlic, and spices.
SIMMER over medium heat 10 minutes or until mixture comes to a boil.
SERVE hot over egg or burrito dishes.
MAKES 2 cups.

Red Chile

MAKING A RISTRA

YOU WILL NEED: ¾ bushel fresh red chile, string or twine, sisal rope.

TIE: cluster of three chiles on string; hold chiles by stems, wrap string around three stems three times.

MAKE: loop over base of stems and pull tightly.

CONTINUE: with three more chile pods. Tie another cluster about 1½ inches from the first cluster and tie string as indicated above.

REPEAT: the above process until all chile has been used; set aside.

TIE: sisal cord to doorknob or nail.

USE: tied chiles; with first three, begin to braid around the sisal rope.

PUSH: chile downward and braid the next three pods until all chile has been used.

HANG: ristra outdoors.

NOTE: It is not necessary to cover red chile with cheesecloth.

Preparation of Dry Red Chile Pods
CHILE CARIBE

Chile caribe, a chile concentrate used as a base for any red chile recipe, makes excellent red chile sauce. It can be frozen in pint containers for later use.

SELECT: one ristra of red chile (2–3 dozen chiles) will make several gallons of sauce. Chiles may also be used as needed off the ristra.

USE: whole pods that are even in color (deep red); free from mold, discoloration, and shriveling; and fresh and pungent smelling.

RINSE: whole pods in cold water.

REMOVE: stems and seeds. Crush pods into small pieces.

PLACE: 14–20 chiles in blender with 2 cups water.

BLEND: at high speed; sauce will resemble tomato sauce in consistency.

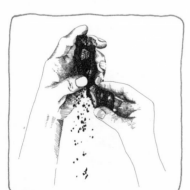

Red Chile Powder

SELECT: 14–20 red chile pods.

REMOVE: stems and seeds.

PLACE: dry pods in blender—about 8 at
a time.

BLEND: to a powder consistency.

STORE: in airtight jars, sealable bags,
or other containers with airtight
lids. (A coffee can will work.)

NOTE: Chile freezes indefinitely in
powder form.

Basic Red Chile Sauce

MADE FROM RED CHILE POWDER

When you don't have chile pods, this is an excellent alternative.

2 tablespoons shortening
2 tablespoons flour
½ cup red chile powder
2 cups cold water
1 teaspoon salt
½ teaspoon garlic salt or garlic
    powder
dash of oregano

HEAT shortening in a stainless steel
    saucepan over medium heat.
STIR in flour to a paste consistency.
COOK for one minute.
ADD red chile powder and cook for an
    additional minute.
ADD cold water gradually and stir
    constantly so that lumps do not
    form.
ADD seasonings.
SIMMER over low heat for 15
    minutes.
USE in any recipe calling for red chile
    sauce.
MAKES about 1 quart.

Fresh Red Chile Sauce

A must in any dish calling for red chile—excellent for enchiladas!

14–20 dry red chile pods
1–2 cups water
½ onion, chopped (optional)
1 tablespoon butter
1 teaspoon salt
1 clove garlic
½ teaspoon oregano

REMOVE chile stems, seeds, and bad spots.
RINSE chiles in cold water.
SOAK chiles in cold water 1–2 hours, or until pods are tender.
PLACE chile in blender with 1–2 cups water.
BLEND chile until it resembles tomato sauce in consistency.
SAUTE onion in butter.
ADD chile and seasonings to onion.
SIMMER ½ hour.
MAKES 1 quart.

EGG DISHES

Huevos Rancheros Tomé Style

4 eggs
2 tablespoons bacon drippings
green chile stew (page 64)

FRY eggs in bacon drippings in
    cast-iron skillet.
POUR hot chile stew over eggs.
SERVE immediately with fresh, hot
    tortillas (page 28) and fried potatoes
    (page 99).
MAKES 2 servings.

Option: Substitute other chile sauces
if chile stew is too meaty for your
taste.

Chile Caribe con Huevos
RED CHILE WITH EGGS

4 eggs
2 tablespoons bacon drippings
red chile sauce (page 48)

FRY or scramble eggs in bacon
    drippings in cast-iron skillet.
POUR hot chile sauce over eggs.
SERVE immediately with hot
    tortillas (page 28).
MAKES 2 servings.

Huevos con Chorizo

EGGS WITH MEXICAN SAUSAGE

2 links chorizo
4 eggs
2 tablespoons milk
1 teaspoon onion salt or 1 small
   onion, chopped
½ cup grated cheddar or Monterey Jack
   cheese
2 tablespoons bacon drippings or oil

SLICE chorizo in nickel-size pieces;
   remove outer skin.
BEAT eggs with milk, onion, and
   grated cheese until foamy.
HEAT bacon drippings or oil in large
   skillet.
BLEND chorizo into egg mixture.
FRY in skillet until lightly browned.
TURN and cook other side, until egg
   and chorizo are done.
SERVE immediately with hot flour
   tortillas.
SERVES 3–4.

Option: Fry two cubed potatoes in oil
until lightly browned; add sliced
chorizo and fry until chorizo is slightly
browned. Add to scrambled eggs.

Southwestern Quiche

1 unbaked pie shell in 9-inch pan
4 eggs
1 teaspoon salt
1 teaspoon onion salt or ½ cup
    minced onion
1 teaspoon red chile powder
1 teaspoon black pepper
1 cup chopped mushrooms
1 cup chopped green chile
2 cups heavy cream or 1 cup
    evaporated milk
1 cup grated Swiss cheese

PREPARE pie crust and place in 9-
    inch pie pan; set aside.
SEPARATE eggs; beat egg yolks; then
    whip egg whites until foamy.
FOLD egg whites into yolks along
    with salt, onion, red chile powder,
    black pepper, chopped mushrooms,
    and green chile.
ADD cream or evaporated milk to
mixture and blend well.
LAYER cheese over bottom of pie
    crust; pour egg mixture into
    pie crust.
BAKE at 425° for 25–30 minutes or
    until quiche is browned and solid.
SERVE hot.
MAKES 6–8 wedges.

Option: Crumble ½ lb. cooked pork
sausage or 1 cup crumbled bacon
(cooked) over top of egg mixture before
baking.

Tortas

This meatless egg dish is often served during Lent.

4 eggs
¼ teaspoon salt
oil for frying
2 cups red chile sauce (page 48)

SEPARATE eggs.
BEAT egg whites until stiff; set aside;
    beat egg yolks and add salt. Add
    yolks to beaten egg whites and
    blend.
DROP egg mixture by tablespoon into
    a hot, oiled skillet.
TURN when browned and cook
    opposite side; drain on absorbent
    towel.
PLACE tortas in a serving dish
    containing red chile sauce.
SERVES 4 individual servings.

Salsa Rancherita Burrito

Salsa Rancherita (page 44)
oil for frying
1 dozen corn tortillas
6 eggs
1 cup grated longhorn cheese
½ cup chopped green chile
1 teaspoon garlic salt
1 teaspoon onion salt or ½ cup
    minced onion
1 large, ripe avocado, peeled and sliced
1 cup shredded lettuce
1 sliced tomato

PREPARE salsa as directed; keep
    warm.
FRY corn tortillas in hot oil; drain on
    absorbent towel.
BEAT eggs, ½ cup cheese, chile, and
    salts or onion; fry in oil remaining
    from tortillas.
STIR egg rapidly in skillet with fork.
    DO NOT brown egg mixture; it
    should be solid and resemble
    popcorn.
PLACE 2 tablespoons egg mixture in
    each corn tortilla. Fold into
    burritos (page 70).
POUR chile sauce over each
    egg/tortilla combination.
GARNISH with avocado, tomato,
    lettuce, and remaining cheese.
SERVE immediately.
MAKES 12 servings.

New Mexican Poached Eggs

Salsa is superb on these poached eggs.

Salsa Rancherita (page 44) or Nana's
    Green Chile Sauce (page 42)
2 tablespoons oil or margarine
8 eggs
½ cup water

PREPARE sauce and keep warm.

HEAT oil or margarine in large skillet.

ADD eggs one at a time. Four eggs
    may be cooked in skillet at once.

ADD ¼ cup water immediately; cover
    skillet; cook over medium heat 2–
    3 minutes or until yolks are firm;
    cook remaining eggs same way.

PLACE eggs on individual serving
    plates and pour ¼ cup sauce over
    each serving.

SERVE immediately with hot flour
    tortillas (page 28).

MAKES 4–6 servings.

Eggs Burrito Style

An economical meatless dish.

6 eggs
¼ cup chopped green chile
1 teaspoon minced onion
½ teaspoon salt
¼ cup milk
¼ teaspoon black pepper
¼ teaspoon garlic salt
6–8 flour tortillas (page 28)
Salsa Rancherita (page 44)
½ cup grated longhorn cheese

MIX together eggs, chile, onion, salt, milk, pepper, and garlic salt.
SCRAMBLE to a firm consistency.
PREPARE Salsa Rancherita in separate saucepan.
WARM tortillas; store-bought tortillas work best for rolling burrito.
PLACE cooked egg mixture in each tortilla and roll jelly-roll fashion.
PLACE egg burritos in an ovenproof dish, seam side down.
SMOTHER each burrito in Salsa Rancherita.
SPRINKLE with grated cheese.
HEAT oven to 350°; place dish in oven 10 minutes or just long enough to melt cheese.
SERVE hot.
MAKES 6–8 servings.

Option: A red chile sauce may be used if desired in place of green chile sauce. You may sprinkle ½ lb. cooked ground sausage atop burritos before baking also.

New Mexican Omelette

8 eggs
2 tablespoons water
½ cup chopped mushrooms
½ cup chopped onion
½ cup chopped green chile
½ cup diced ham
½ cup grated Swiss cheese or
    Monterey Jack cheese
2 tablespoons oil or margarine

BEAT eggs in large bowl; add water, mushrooms, onion, chile, ham, and cheese; blend well.
HEAT oil or margarine in large skillet.
POUR egg mixture into skillet and cook until solid.
SERVE immediately with hot flour tortillas.
MAKES 6–8 servings.

MAIN DISHES

Green Chile Enchilada Casserole

1½ lbs. of ground meat (beef, venison, elk, or combination) or shredded chicken
½ cup chopped onion
2 cloves garlic, minced
1 pkg. (12 count) corn tortillas
oil for frying
2 10¾ oz. cans cream of mushroom soup or chicken broth
1 cup chopped green chile
1 small can chopped ripe olives
1 lb. grated longhorn cheese

BROWN meat; drain fat; add onion and garlic; cook 5 minutes; set aside.
FRY tortillas in oil; drain on paper towel; set aside.
MIX soup and chile to make sauce; add olives.
LAYER meat, ⅓ of cheese, tortillas, another ⅓ of cheese, sauce, and remaining cheese in baking dish.
COVER casserole with foil.
BAKE at 350° 35–45 minutes.
MAKES 4–6 servings.

Carne Asada con Chile Verde

GREEN CHILE BEEF STEAKS

1 large round steak (about 2 lbs.) salt pepper flour cooking oil ½ cup chopped green chile 1 cup Monterey Jack cheese, grated	CUT steak into 4 serving-size portions. POUND steak on both sides. SALT and pepper to taste. DREDGE in flour. PAN fry in hot oil until tender. DRAIN on paper towel. PLACE steaks on cookie sheet. SMOTHER with chopped green chile and top with cheese. BAKE at 350° until cheese melts (about 10 minutes). MAKES 4 servings.

Green Chile Stew

A hearty cold-day stew!

1 lb. ground beef or 1 lb. diced pork
4 small potatoes, peeled and diced*
2 cups green chile, chopped
1 cup stewed tomatoes, chopped
1 teaspoon garlic salt
1 teaspoon onion salt
2 cups water

BROWN beef or pork and potatoes
    together.
STIR constantly to prevent sticking.
DRAIN excess fat.
ADD green chile, tomatoes, salts, and
    water.
BRING to a boil and simmer 15–20
    minutes.
SERVE immediately with flour
    tortillas.
MAKES 4–6 ½ cup servings.

*Potatoes may be boiled before using
to ensure that they cook thoroughly.

Red Chile Stew

1 lb. ground beef
2 small potatoes, peeled and diced*
2–3 tablespoons red chile powder
1 teaspoon garlic salt
1 teaspoon salt
½ cup tomato sauce
2 cups water

BROWN ground beef with potatoes
    until cooked; stir constantly to
    prevent sticking; drain excess fat.
ADD chile powder, salts, tomato sauce,
    and water.
SIMMER 20–30 minutes.
SERVE hot with flour tortillas.
MAKES 4–6 ½ cup servings.

*Potatoes may be boiled before using
to ensure that they cook thoroughly.

Green Chile Enchiladas

1 dozen corn tortillas
oil
green chile stew (page 64)
2 tablespoons cornstarch
¼ cup cold water
2 cups grated cheddar or longhorn
    cheese
chopped tomato, shredded lettuce,
    diced onion

FRY corn tortillas in hot oil; keep
    tortillas soft; do not overcook.
DRAIN on absorbent towel.
PREPARE green chile stew and keep
    warm over low heat.
ADD cornstarch to water and then add
    to chile stew to thicken.
PLACE ¼ cup thickened chile stew
    on each tortilla on baking sheet
    or dish.
SPRINKLE with grated cheese.
PLACE tortillas in stacks of 3 layers,
    each topped with chile and cheese.
BAKE at 350° for 10 to 15 minutes or
    until cheese melts.
GARNISH with tomato, lettuce, and
    onion.
MAKES 4 3-layer servings or 12 rolled
    enchiladas.

Option: Enchiladas may be rolled
rather than layered.

Red Chile Enchiladas

Serve a fried egg on top of these if you like.

12 corn tortillas
oil
1 lb. longhorn cheese, grated
2 chopped onions
red chile sauce (pages 48, 49)
1½ cups shredded lettuce

FRY corn tortillas in hot oil; drain on
  paper towel.
SPRINKLE each tortilla with cheese
  and onions.
ROLL jelly-roll fashion.
PLACE seam down in large baking
  dish; top with red chile sauce and
  sprinkle with more onions and
  cheese, if desired.
BAKE at 350° until cheese melts, about
  10–15 minutes.
SERVE with lettuce and Spanish
  Rice (page 98).
MAKES 12 enchiladas; serves 4.

Option: Tortillas may be layered in
stacks of three for flat enchiladas
rather than rolled.

Green Chile Sour Cream Enchiladas

1 dozen corn tortillas
oil
green chile sauce with pork (page 41)
2 cups sour cream
½ cup chopped green chile
½ cup minced onion
2 cups grated longhorn cheese
2 tomatoes, cut into wedges

FRY corn tortillas in hot oil; keep tortillas soft; do not overcook.
DRAIN on paper towel.
PREPARE green chile sauce and keep warm over low heat.
BLEND sour cream, green chile, and onion; set aside.
PLACE tortillas in stacks of 3 layers, each topped with chile sauce, 1 tablespoon sour cream mixture, and cheese.
TOP layer should end with sour cream mixture and cheese.
GARNISH with tomato wedges.
SERVE immediately.
MAKES 4 3-layer servings or 12 rolled enchiladas.

NOTE: Keep chile sauce hot so cheese will melt; this will eliminate necessity of placing in oven.

Options: Cooked chicken may be substituted for pork meat in chile sauce. Enchiladas may be rolled rather than layered.

Crockpot Chile Stew

1 whole chicken, cut up
4–6 cups water
1 10¾ oz. can cream of mushroom or
    cream of chicken soup
12 corn tortillas, cut in strips
1 teaspoon garlic salt
1 pkg. chicken gravy mix
½ cup chopped green chile

COOK chicken in crockpot with water
    to cover, about 4 hours.
ADD remaining ingredients the last
    half hour of cooking.
ALLOW to boil until tortillas are
    tender.
SERVE over rice.
MAKES 5–6 servings.

Carne Adovada

RED CHILE PORK STEAKS

red chile sauce (page 48)
6 pork steaks
½ teaspoon garlic salt
pepper
1 tablespoon oregano
¼ teaspoon coriander (optional)
2 cloves garlic, minced

PREPARE chile sauce as directed.
SEASON pork steaks with garlic salt,
    pepper, oregano, and coriander.
MARINATE pork steaks in chile sauce
    with minced garlic cloves
    overnight, in glass dish.
FRY pork steaks in fat until well done
    or bake covered in oven 1 hour
    at 325°.
SERVE with rice and hot flour
    tortillas (page 28).
MAKES 4–6 servings.

Burritos Smothered in Green Chile

Simplemente delicioso (simply delicious!)

GREEN CHILE SAUCE
2 lbs. cubed pork
1 medium diced onion
2 cloves minced garlic
1 teaspoon salt
¼ teaspoon oregano
4 cups water
4 fresh diced tomatoes
1 cup chopped green chile

BROWN pork; drain excess fat.
ADD remaining ingredients, except tomatoes and chile.
SIMMER for 1½ hours or until meat is tender.
ADD tomatoes and chile and simmer about 15 minutes longer.

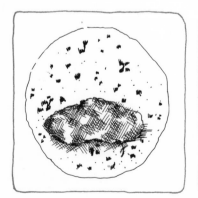 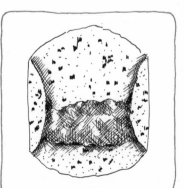 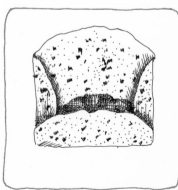

BURRITOS
refried beans (page 105 or 1 28 oz.
   can)
1 chopped onion
1 lb. longhorn cheese, shredded
12 flour tortillas (page 28)

SPREAD mixture of refried beans,
   onions, and cheese on each tortilla,
   very thin. Bring edges of tortilla to
   center, overlap one edge over the
   other, or roll jelly-roll fashion.
PLACE seam down in a large square
   baking dish.
POUR chile sauce over burritos.
SPRINKLE with extra shredded
   cheese.
BAKE at 350° 10–15 minutes or until
   cheese melts.
MAKES 12.

Burrito Supreme

*The basic burrito garnished with guacamole becomes
a Burrito Supreme!*

Salsa Verde con Carne (page 41)
12 flour tortillas (page 28)
1 lb. longhorn cheese, grated
2 large onions, diced
½ head lettuce, shredded
guacamole (page 16)
1 large tomato, cut in wedges

SPREAD ¼ cup sauce along outer
  edge of each tortilla; sprinkle with
  cheese and onion.
ROLL jelly-roll style or into thirds.
PLACE seam down on serving plates.
BAKE at 350° for 10 minutes.
SMOTHER with extra chile sauce.
GARNISH with lettuce, guacamole,
  tomato wedges, and extra cheese
  and onion.
MAKES 12.

Southwestern Tamale Pie

1 lb. ground beef
1 small onion, diced
1 10¾ oz. can cream of chicken soup
1 10¾ oz. can Golden Mushroom soup
1 cup evaporated milk
1 4 oz. can taco sauce
1½ cups chopped green chile
1 dozen corn tortillas
1½ cups grated cheddar or Monterey Jack cheese

BROWN meat with onion in large skillet; drain excess fat. Add soups, milk, taco sauce, and green chile.
SIMMER all ingredients together about 10 minutes.
CUT corn tortillas into strips. (Tortillas do not need to be fried.)
LAYER on bottom of 2-quart casserole dish with meat mixture and cheese; continue alternating layers; top layer should end with cheese.
COVER casserole and bake at 350° for 1 hour.
MAKES 5–6 servings.

Option: Use 1 cooked, boned, diced chicken in place of ground beef.

Chimichangas

12 flour tortillas (page 28)
meat filling (see below)
1½–2 cups shredded longhorn
    cheese and lettuce
oil
½ pint sour cream
guacamole (page 16)

MEAT FILLING
1½ lbs. ground beef
1 clove garlic, minced
¼ cup dry minced onion
1 teaspoon oregano
¼ teaspoon cumin

BROWN meat with garlic and onion.
ADD seasonings and stir well.
SIMMER over medium heat about 10
    minutes.

SPOON 3 tablespoons meat filling
    and cheese in center of each
    tortilla; fold tortilla by bringing
    edges to center and overlapping one
    edge over the other; secure with
    toothpick.
FRY tortillas in 1 inch hot oil; fry 2
    minutes on each side.
SPREAD sour cream over each and
    top with guacamole.
MAKES 12.

Chile Rellenos

These are best with fresh green chiles.

4 eggs
¾ teaspoon baking powder
4 tablespoons flour
¼ teaspoon salt
12 large, peeled, whole green chiles
    with stems
1 lb. longhorn cheese, cut into strips
oil for frying

BEAT eggs until foamy; add baking
    powder, flour, and salt. Set batter
    aside.
SLIT each chile open lengthwise below
    stem and insert cheese.
DIP stuffed chiles in batter and fry in
    oil in cast-iron skillet until golden
    brown.
DRAIN on paper towel.
MAKES 12.

Option: For heavier batter, add ¼ cup
yellow cornmeal.

Sweet Chile Rellenos

Sweet chile rellenos are served at Christmas gatherings and wedding feasts.

1 egg
¼ cup milk
2 lbs. boiled pork, diced
1 cup chopped green chile
½ cup brown sugar
1 cup raisins, finely chopped
¼ teaspoon nutmeg
¼ teaspoon cinnamon
piñon nuts, shelled (optional)
½ cup flour
¼ teaspoon salt
oil for frying

BEAT egg and milk together; in separate bowl, combine meat, chile, sugar, raisins, spices, and nuts.
ADD 2 tablespoons of egg mixture; coat hands with flour and shape mixture into ovals about small egg size.
ADD flour and salt to egg mixture; dip each oval in this mixture.
DEEP fry until golden brown; drain on absorbent towel.
SERVE with caramel syrup, below.
MAKES 1 dozen.

CARAMEL SYRUP
¼ cup brown sugar
1 cup water
1 teaspoon vanilla extract
1 teaspoon cinnamon

HEAT sugar until brown; add other ingredients and boil several minutes until mixture reaches syrup consistency.
POUR over chile rellenos.

Mama Trini's Stuffed Green Chile

When the season for roasting chile arrives, Mamacita's children gather to feast on this savory dish.

8 fresh roasted and peeled green chiles
½ cup grated mozzarella cheese
2 medium fresh tomatoes, finely
    chopped
½–1 teaspoon garlic salt

SLIT each chile and stuff with cheese
    and tomatoes.
SPRINKLE with garlic salt.
PLACE stuffed chiles, in single layer
    only, in 8″ × 13″ baking dish.
BAKE at 350° until cheese melts, about
    10–15 minutes.
MAKES 8.

NOTE: This recipe works very well in a microwave oven.

Beefed-Up Chile Casserole

A quick and easy chile supper in one dish.

1 lb. ground beef ½ cup chopped onion ½ cup chopped green chile 1 cup (8 oz. can) tomato sauce 2 teaspoons red chile powder 1 teaspoon garlic salt 1 can (8 oz. size) refrigerator buttermilk biscuits 1 cup shredded Monterey Jack or cheddar cheese	BROWN beef and onion in large skillet; drain fat. STIR in chile, tomato sauce, chile powder, and garlic salt. SIMMER while preparing dough. SEPARATE biscuit dough into 10 biscuits; divide these into 20 biscuits. LINE 7″ × 11″ baking dish with 10 biscuits. SPRINKLE with ½ cup cheese. SPOON meat mixture over dough and cheese. TOP with remaining biscuits and cheese. BAKE at 375° for 25–30 minutes or until biscuits are brown. MAKES 4–6 servings.

Tostadas

guacamole (page 16)
1 pkg. (12 count) tostada shells or
    12 corn tortillas fried until crisp
1 lb. ground beef
¼ teaspoon garlic salt
¼ teaspoon onion salt
¼ teaspoon cumin
refried beans (page 105 or 1 large can)
1 lb. longhorn cheese, grated
salsa pequin (page 43)
shredded lettuce
diced tomatoes

PREPARE guacamole; set aside.
IF using corn tortillas, fry until crisp
    and drain on paper towel.
BROWN meat with seasonings; drain
    off excess fat. Set meat aside.
SPREAD thin layer of refried beans on
    each tortilla or tostada shell.
SPRINKLE meat over beans.
TOP each tostada with cheese.
BAKE at 350° for 15–20 minutes or
    until cheese melts.
SERVE immediately, garnished with
    salsa pequin, guacamole, lettuce,
    and tomatoes.
MAKES 12.

Chuletas Españolas

A prize-winning pork chop recipe! Try simmering this all day in your crockpot.

6 pork chops
salt and pepper to taste
red chile sauce (pages 48, 49)
1 teaspoon onion salt
1 teaspoon cumin
1 teaspoon oregano
2 cloves garlic, sliced

SEASON chops with salt and pepper.
BROWN chops in small amount of
    fat.
ADD seasonings to red chile.
SIMMER meat in sauce 1–2 hours or
    until very tender.
SERVE with rice.
MAKES 6 servings.

Option: For a delicious accompaniment to Chuletas Españolas, prepare rice using chicken broth in place of water and onion salt. Top with butter and parsley flakes.

Mutton Stew

A traditional and economical stew.

2 lbs. mutton, cubed
6 cups water
6 potatoes, peeled and cubed
1 onion, diced
1 clove garlic, diced
½ cup chopped green chile
1 tablespoon salt
1 teaspoon pepper

PLACE all ingredients in large pot.
BRING to a boil over medium heat;
then cook over low heat for 1–2
hours.
ADD salt and pepper last half hour of
cooking.
SERVE hot with fry bread (page 31).
MAKES 4–6 1-cup servings.

Southwestern Green Chile with Rice Soup

1 lb. lean ground beef or cubed pork
3 cups cooked rice
1 cup chopped green chile
1 teaspoon garlic salt
1½ cups water

BROWN beef or pork until well done;
drain excess fat.
ADD rice, chile, water, and salt.
SIMMER about 20 minutes.
SERVE hot with flour tortillas (page
28).
MAKES 4–5 1-cup servings.

New Mexican Crepes

salsa rancherita (page 44)
2 cups cooked, shredded chicken
1 cup grated Swiss or Monterey Jack
  cheese (optional)

CREPES:
4 eggs
1½ cups milk
2 tablespoons oil
1 cup flour
½ teaspoon salt
½ teaspoon baking powder

PREHEAT griddle to medium heat.
BEAT eggs slightly; add remaining
  crepe ingredients and beat until
  smooth.

PREPARE salsa as directed and add
  chicken. Keep warm over low heat.
GREASE griddle thoroughly; pour ⅛
  cup (2 tablespoons) batter onto
  griddle; tilt griddle slightly so that
  batter covers pan.
TURN after 2–3 minutes when batter
  is solid and other side is lightly
  browned.
PLACE ¼ cup salsa in center of each
  cooked crepe; roll crepe loosely.
POUR ¼ cup salsa over crepe; garnish
  with grated cheese, if desired.
CREPES may be kept warm in oven or
  microwave.
MAKES 6–8 crepes.

Gorditas

FAT ONES

These fried masa cups filled with a mixture of chorizo and beans are very popular in southern New Mexico.

*DOUGH
2 cups masa harina
1 cup water
oil for frying

*FILLING
chorizo con frijoles (page 104)
green chile sauce (page 44)

*GARNISHES
grated Swiss cheese
guacamole (page 16)
shredded lettuce
tomato wedges

COMBINE masa and water to form a
   soft, workable dough.
ROLL dough with hands to form egg-
   size balls. Place each ball between
   2 pieces of waxed paper or plastic
   wrap and roll to form a 3-inch
   disk.
PLACE on warm, ungreased griddle for
   10 seconds on each side. Fold up
   edges while still warm to form a
   cup shape.
DEEP fry for 2 minutes; drain on
   paper towel.
FILL each cup with chorizo con
   frijoles.
SPOON chile sauce over chorizo
   mixture.
SERVE with garnishes.
MAKES 4–6.

Libby's Vermicelli Español

Delicious with red chile and pork.

2 tablespoons bacon drippings or oil
1 pkg. coiled vermicelli
1 cup (8 oz. can) tomato sauce
1 cup water
1–2 teaspoons onion salt
½ teaspoon garlic salt

HEAT bacon drippings or oil over medium heat in large skillet.

PLACE vermicelli in skillet and turn constantly until brown, but do not burn.

TURN burner off. Add tomato sauce but *be sure to cover skillet as soon as you have added tomato sauce because sauce will splatter.*

ADD water and salts to taste; simmer, covered, over low heat until liquid is completely evaporated and vermicelli are tender. Add more water as necessary to keep vermicelli from drying out or burning.

MAKES 3–4 servings.

Chalupas

A guacamole garnish will make these extra fancy.

1 dozen corn tortillas
oil for frying
2 cups refried beans (page 105 or 1
    large can)
salsa pequin (page 43)
1½ cups longhorn cheese, shredded
1½ cups finely chopped lettuce,
    onion, and tomato

FRY tortillas in oil until crisp. Form
    into boat shapes.
DRAIN on paper towels.
SPREAD refried beans on each tortilla
    boat. Add salsa, cheese, tomato,
    onion, and lettuce.
SERVE immediately.
MAKES 12.

NOTE: A handy way to make the boat
shapes is to fry tortillas until pliable,
drain on paper towels, and place in
muffin tins in 350° oven until crisp.

Red Chile Tamales

Tamales are served traditionally during Christmas holidays, wedding feasts, and other special events.

*MEAT PREPARATION
5–6 lbs. pork loin with fat
2–4 quarts water

BOIL pork loin in water in large
    kettle; replenish water as
    necessary. Cook over medium heat
    4–5 hours. When pork is cooked,
    cool. Reserve liquid from cooking
    pork for dough. Trim fat. Reserve
    fat for dough.
SHRED meat and set aside.

*RED CHILE PREPARATION
2 dozen red chile pods (dry)
3 cups water

SOAK and wash chile pods.
CRUMBLE chile pods and remove
    stems and seeds. Soak chile in
    warm water ½ hour.
DRAIN; place 1 cup pods in blender
    with ½ cup fresh water.
BLEND 15–20 seconds. Repeat
    process until all chile is liquid.
SET aside.

*CHILE/MEAT PREPARATION
shredded pork
blended red chile
1 teaspoon garlic salt
1 teaspoon onion salt
1 teaspoon salt

MIX pieces of pork with red chile
  liquid. Place in large skillet; add
  salts. Bring to a boil over medium
  heat. Simmer over low heat 20
  minutes.
DO NOT let chile/meat mixture dry
  out; it should be kept juicy. Add
  more water if necessary.

*MASA PREPARATION
5–6 cups masa harina
2 cups shortening (including reserved
    fat from cooked pork loin)
2 teaspoons salt
liquid from cooked pork (lukewarm)
1–2 cups water

IN large bowl, cream shortening and
  pork fat into masa harina.
ADD salt and liquid; mix dough.
ADD more masa harina or liquid as
  necessary to form solid dough;
  dough texture should be
  shiny—not dry.

(continued next page)

Red Chile Tamales, continued

*CORN HUSK PREPARATION
3–4 dozen dry corn husks

SOAK corn husks in hot water; wash thoroughly; remove corn hairs from each husk.

SEPARATE corn husks; dry on paper towel. Open each husk; 1–2 corn husks can be used together by overlapping; the palm of your hand should fit comfortably in husks.

*FINAL PREPARATION
PLACE 3-inch ball of masa on each corn husk. Flatten with palm of hand over center of husk until dough is ¼–½″ thick and 4″ in diameter. Place 1–2 tablespoons chile/meat mixture onto dough in center. Roll husk across width along with dough and meat mixture; fold bottom of husk so that chile does not spill out. Top of tamale is left open for steam to escape when cooking.

*STEAMING TAMALES

POUR 2 cups water in bottom of pressure cooker or large kettle with lid and steaming rack so that tamales do not actually touch bottom of pan and water can circulate.

STAND tamales upright in pan, closely packed so they will stay folded.

COVER and steam over low to medium heat.

IMPORTANT: Make sure there is always sufficient water in bottom of pan to avoid burning tamales.

DEPENDING on how many tamales are in your pot, steaming time will vary. A dozen tamales must be steamed for an hour. Three dozen will need three hours.

PRESSURE COOKER: 1½ hours at 10 lbs. pressure.

MAKES 3–4 dozen.

PREPARED tamales freeze well after they are completely cooled. Wrapped in double aluminum foil, they can be stored frozen 2–3 months.

Chicos

Chicos are a popular Northern New Mexico dish.

3 cups chicos
12 cups water
1½ lbs. cubed pork
1 diced onion
1 clove minced garlic
6 crushed red chile pods
½ teaspoon oregano
3 teaspoons salt
½ teaspoon black pepper

WASH chicos thoroughly; soak overnight; drain when ready to use.

BOIL chicos until tender about 3½ hours in 6 cups water.

BROWN pork; add onion and garlic; saute together until tender; drain excess fat.

ADD pork, chile pods, oregano, salt, pepper, and 6 cups water to cooked chicos.

SIMMER for 1 hour or until the meat and corn are tender.

MAKES 2 quarts.

NOTE: Chicos may be cooked in a pressure cooker for 45 minutes at about 15 lbs. pressure.

Posole

HOMINY STEW

Posole, or hominy stew, has long been a traditional stew among both the Indian and Spanish cultures. It is popular at Christmas and New Year's celebrations.

*POSOLE MIXTURE
2 pkgs. frozen posole
12 cups water
1–2 teaspoons salt
1 tablespoon coriander seed
4 cloves garlic

RINSE posole in cold water.
PLACE all ingredients in large kettle.
BOIL mixture until posole kernels
    burst open (3–4 hours).

*MEAT MIXTURE
4 lbs. pork loin
6 cloves garlic
12 cups water
2 tablespoons salt
1 teaspoon oregano
1 teaspoon onion salt

CUT pork loin into 1-inch cubes.
BOIL ingredients in a kettle until
    meat is tender, about 4 hours.
POUR posole mixture into meat
    mixture and simmer for 1 hour.
SERVE posole with red chile sauce
    (pages 48, 49).
MAKES 6–8 individual servings.

Option: Tripe or pork skins (½ lb., cut into squares) may be added to hominy at beginning of cooking, if desired.

Flautas

FLUTES

Flautas resemble rolled tacos. They are a delicate blend of chicken, onion, chile pequín, and seasonings, deep fried and topped with sour cream and guacamole.

3 chicken breasts
1 pkg. corn tortillas
oil for frying
¼ cup minced onion
¼ cup chile pequín
onion salt
garlic salt
guacamole (page 16)
tomato wedges (optional)
1 pint sour cream

BOIL chicken until tender, about 1 hour. Bone chicken; chop; set aside.
FRY corn tortillas in 1 inch of oil for 5 seconds on each side.
DRAIN on paper towel.
PLACE chicken on one side of tortilla, sprinkle with onion, chile pequin, and salts.
ROLL jelly-roll fashion.
SECURE with toothpick.
FRY 1–2 minutes until crisp.
DRAIN on paper towel; place in a warm oven until serving time.
SERVE topped with guacamole and sour cream. Guacamole should be mixed into sour cream for use as topping.
GARNISH with tomato wedges if you wish.
MAKES 12.

Option: 2 lbs. cooked beef brisket or 2 lbs. cooked pork may be substituted for chicken, if desired.

New Mexican Pizza

This is also known as a sopaipilla compuesta and as a Navajo taco.

sopaipillas (page 30)
2–3 cups green chile stew (page 64)
1 cup grated Monterey Jack cheese
diced tomato, onion, and lettuce

PREPARE sopaipillas as directed; fry and drain on paper towel. You may prefer to make these round rather than square sopaipillas.

PREPARE green chile stew and simmer; place ¼ to ½ cup chile stew over each cooled sopaipilla; sprinkle with grated cheese.

GARNISH with tomato, onion, and lettuce.

SERVE immediately.

MAKES 1 dozen.

Tacos

Easy and tasty, tacos can also be eaten as leftovers for next day's lunch!

1 dozen corn tortillas or 1 dozen commercial taco shells
oil for frying
1 lb. ground beef
2–3 medium potatoes, peeled, diced, and boiled*
½ teaspoon onion salt
½ teaspoon garlic salt
¼ teaspoon cumin
dash of pepper
1½ cups salsa pequin (page 43)
2 cups shredded cheddar or longhorn cheese
1 cup shredded lettuce
1 tomato, diced
1 onion, diced

FRY corn tortillas in hot oil; fold in half and fry until crisp.
IF using commercial taco shells, do not fry.
BROWN beef in large skillet; drain excess fat. Add potatoes and seasonings.
PLACE 2 tablespoons meat mixture in each shell.
SPRINKLE with grated cheese.
ADD 1 tablespoon salsa to each taco (or 1 teaspoon for milder flavor).
GARNISH with tomato, lettuce, onion, and cheese.
SERVE immediately.
MAKES 12.

*Leftover baked potatoes may be substituted after peeling skin.

VEGETABLES

Garden-Fresh Salad

1 medium head iceberg lettuce
1 head leaf lettuce
1 ripe avocado, cut in wedges
1 cauliflower, torn into buds
2 tomatoes, cut in wedges
4 radishes, sliced
1 zucchini, sliced
1 bell pepper, chopped
1 red onion, sliced

WASH all vegetables and pat dry.
RESERVE enough leaf lettuce to line salad bowl.
TEAR remaining lettuce into bite-size portions.
COMBINE all vegetables and toss gently.
SERVE with favorite salad dressing.
MAKES 3–4 servings.

Spanish Slaw

Your food processor will be helpful for shredding.

2 cups shredded cabbage
½ cup shredded red cabbage
1 onion, diced or shredded
1 carrot, shredded
1 clove garlic, minced

COMBINE all vegetables until well mixed.
STIR dressing into vegetables.

*DRESSING
½ cup mayonnaise
¼ cup vinegar
3 tablespoons sugar

COMBINE ingredients.
CHILL until ready to serve.

Pinto Bean–Taco Salad

Great for a summer picnic!

2 cups shredded lettuce
2 cups cooked, drained, cooled pinto
  beans (page 103)
1½ cups cooked ground beef, drained
  and cooled
1 medium tomato, diced
1½ cups shredded longhorn cheese
1 small bag corn tortilla chips,
  crushed
½ cup chopped green chile
4 tablespoons mayonnaise
1 teaspoon onion salt or 1 small
  onion, minced
1 avocado, sliced
1 bell pepper, sliced
black olives, sliced

PLACE lettuce and beans in large salad
  bowl.
ADD beef, tomato, cheese, and tortilla
  chips. Toss.
MIX chile with mayonnaise and onion
  salt or onion. Use chile mixture as
  salad dressing.
CHILL dressed salad several hours.
GARNISH with avocado, bell pepper,
  and olive slices.
MAKES 4–6 servings.

Spanish Rice

A side dish of rice is delicious with red or green chile enchiladas.

2 tablespoons bacon drippings or oil
1½ cups uncooked long-grain rice
1 8 oz. can tomato sauce
2–3 cups water
¼ teaspoon garlic salt or 1 clove garlic, minced
½ teaspoon onion salt or 1 small onion, minced

HEAT bacon drippings or oil over medium heat in large skillet.
ADD rice, stirring constantly until rice is lightly browned. *Be careful not to burn rice.*
TURN burner off. Add tomato sauce, water, and salts or garlic and onion.
COVER immediately. Simmer over low heat until all liquid is evaporated and rice, onion, and garlic are tender, 25–30 minutes. Add more water only if necessary to prevent drying.
SERVE immediately.
MAKES 4–6 ½-cup servings.

Option: Add ½ cup diced green and red bell pepper to rice before simmering.

Papas Fritas

FRIED POTATOES

Delicious with eggs or a meat dish at any meal.

8 potatoes
2 tablespoons bacon drippings or oil
2 large onions, minced
1 teaspoon salt
½ teaspoon black pepper

WASH and peel potatoes; slice very thin.
HEAT drippings or oil over medium high heat in skillet.
COOK potatoes until golden brown on one side.
TURN potatoes and smother with onion.
TURN once more to mix potato and onion.
SEASON with salt and pepper; serve immediately.
MAKES 6–8 servings.

Taco Frijoles para los Niños

BEAN TACO FOR THE LITTLE ONES

Easy tacos; delicious for children and adults.

1 pkg. nacho-style chips cooked pinto beans (page 103) shredded lettuce 1 lb. shredded longhorn cheese 1 large diced onion salsa pequin, if desired (page 43)	PLACE chips on bottom of individual serving bowls. PLACE beans in individual bowls. TOP with lettuce, cheese, and onion. SPRINKLE with salsa pequin, if desired. SERVE hot. MAKES 8 servings.

Zucchini and Corn

CALABACITAS CON MAIZ

2 medium zucchini
2 tablespoons bacon drippings or oil
kernels from 6 ears fresh corn, or one
    16 oz. can, drained
1 small onion, minced

WASH zucchini thoroughly and dice. Do
    not peel.
HEAT bacon drippings or oil in large
    skillet.
SIMMER zucchini, corn, and onion in
    covered skillet over low heat 15–
    20 minutes until tender and lightly
    browned.
SERVE hot with tortillas (page 28).
MAKES 3–4 servings.

Option: Add ½ cup chopped green
chile.

Spinach

QUELITES

4 slices bacon, chopped
6 tablespoons minced onion
4 cups raw spinach
¼ cup cooked pinto beans (page 103)

COOK bacon and remove from skillet.
SAUTE onion in bacon drippings until transparent. Drain off drippings.
ADD bacon, spinach, and beans and simmer over low heat for 10 minutes.
SERVE immediately with hot flour tortillas (page 28).
MAKES 4–6 ½-cup servings.

Pinto Beans

FRIJOLES

Delicioso—with red or green chile and hot flour tortillas!

2 cups raw pinto beans
1 quart cold water
2 tablespoons bacon drippings or
   shortening
1 tablespoon salt

CLEAN raw beans (make sure there
   are no rocks with them).
RINSE thoroughly with cool water
   several times.
DRAIN and place beans in stainless 2-
   quart pan; add 1 quart cold water
   and bacon drippings or shortening.
COOK, covered, over low to medium
   heat 2–3 hours; add water as
   necessary to keep beans from
   drying; during last hour of cooking,
   add salt.
MAKES 1–1½ quarts beans.

NOTE: 1 clove garlic may be boiled
with beans to prevent bloaty effect.

Chorizo con Frijoles

MEXICAN SAUSAGE WITH BEANS

Chorizo and beans rolled in a flour tortilla make a tantalizing burrito.

1–2 tablespoons bacon drippings or
   shortening
2 chorizo links, skinned and sliced
2 cups cooked pinto beans (page 103)

HEAT fat in large skillet.
SLICE chorizo in nickel-size pieces.
FRY over medium heat until chorizo
   browns and beans thicken.
SERVE immediately with hot flour
   tortillas (page 28).
MAKES 3–4 half-cup servings.

Refried Beans

FRIJOLES REFRITOS

Refried beans are an accompaniment to many Southwestern main dishes.

1 quart cooked pinto beans (page 103)
2 tablespoons bacon drippings or shortening
1 cup grated cheddar or longhorn cheese

PREPARE pinto beans as directed, *except* simmer last hour until most of the juice is evaporated and beans are almost dry.

DRAIN any excess liquid.

HEAT bacon drippings or shortening in large skillet.

MASH beans and add to hot fat.

FRY over medium heat until beans are thick and bubbly.

SERVE immediately sprinkled with grated cheddar or longhorn cheese.

MAKES 4–6 ½-cup servings.

Papas con Chile Colorado
POTATOES WITH RED CHILE

Good with eggs.

2 tablespoons oil
4 cups cubed potatoes
2 tablespoons flour
1 tablespoon ground red chile powder
1 teaspoon salt
4 cups water
1 clove garlic, minced

HEAT oil in large skillet.
ADD potatoes and cook until tender; stir to prevent sticking. Remove potatoes.
ADD flour; brown lightly.
ADD chile powder, salt, and water; stir together.
ADD garlic and potatoes. Simmer 15–20 minutes.
MAKES 4 servings.

Papas con Chile Verde
GREEN CHILE POTATOES

2 tablespoons oil
4 cups cubed potatoes
¼ cup finely chopped onion
¼ cup chopped green chile
1 clove garlic, minced
1 teaspoon salt
4 cups water

HEAT oil in large skillet.
ADD potatoes and onion.
FRY until onion is transparent and potatoes are tender; stir to prevent sticking; add chile, garlic, and salt.
STIR together; add water.
SIMMER 20 minutes or until potatoes are tender.
MAKES 4 servings.

MICROWAVE
ADAPTATIONS

Nachos

1 8 oz. pkg. tortilla chips
1½ cups shredded longhorn or
    cheddar cheese
¼ cup chopped green chile
1 2 oz. can sliced olives

ON platter, place tortilla chips in
    single layer.
SPRINKLE with cheese and top with
    ¼ teaspoon chile and olives.
MICROWAVE 3–4 minutes.
MAKES appetizers sufficient for 6–8
    people.

Enchiladas

enchiladas (pages 66-68)

PREPARE enchiladas according to
    recipe, but
MICROWAVE 1–2 minutes.
MAKES 1 dozen.

NOTE: Onions cook and cheese melts
    very quickly.

Confetti Chile Omelette

Top this with your favorite salsa.

*EGG MIXTURE
4 eggs
¼ teaspoon salt
⅛ teaspoon onion salt
⅛ teaspoon garlic salt
1½ tablespoons butter

SEPARATE eggs. Beat whites until
   fluffy but not dry.
BEAT yolks with seasonings; fold in
   egg whites carefully with rubber
   spatula. Set aside.
MELT butter in microwave on high for
   30 seconds in glass pie plate. Add
   egg mixture.
MICROWAVE at 50% power for 5
   minutes.
LIFT edges and cook 2–4 minutes.

*FILLING
½ cup shredded longhorn cheese
¼ cup chopped green chile
¼ cup chopped ham

SPRINKLE mixture of cheese, chile,
   and ham on half of the omelette.
   Loosen omelette. Fold in half.
SMOTHER with salsa (page 44) and
   more cheese if desired.

Burritos

12 flour tortillas (page 28)
burrito filling (page 71)
burrito sauce (page 70)
1 cup shredded longhorn cheese

PLACE burrito filling on one end of tortilla.
SPRINKLE with cheese. Roll. Top with burrito sauce. Sprinkle with more cheese.
MICROWAVE 2–3 minutes.
MAKES 12.

Dorito Casserole

green chile enchilada casserole (page 62)
1 pkg. Doritos (use in place of corn tortillas)
1 cup sliced olives

PREPARE casserole as directed, but substitute Doritos for corn tortillas and sprinkle olives between layers.
MICROWAVE 5–10 minutes or until cheese is thoroughly melted.
MAKES 3–4 servings.

NOTE: Other corn tortilla casseroles, such as the tamale pie on page 73, can be prepared in the microwave.

Zesty Appetizer Meatballs

Prepare these ahead of time. They freeze well and only take minutes to reheat.

1 egg
⅓ cup milk
⅓ cup dry bread crumbs
1 tablespoon minced onion
1 lb. ground beef
¼ cup chopped green chile

COMBINE all ingredients and mix thoroughly. Form into 1-inch balls.

PLACE on a rack and microwave on high for 5 minutes. Drain excess fat.

SERVE immediately or freeze after cooling, if desired.

MAKES appetizers sufficient for 6–8 people.

DESSERTS

Mama's Spice Cake

Potatoes are the secret ingredient in this recipe, making an extra-moist cake.

2¼ cups flour
2 teaspoons baking powder
1 teaspoon cinnamon
1 teaspoon nutmeg
1 cup shortening or margarine
2 cups sugar
2 eggs
1½ sq. unsweetened chocolate,
    melted, or 4½ tablespoons cocoa
1 cup unseasoned mashed potatoes
1 cup cold coffee
1 teaspoon vanilla
1 cup chopped walnuts

SIFT dry ingredients; set aside.
CREAM shortening with sugar.
ADD eggs and beat well.
ADD chocolate or cocoa and potatoes.
BLEND well and add dry ingredients
    alternately with coffee and vanilla,
    beating until smooth after each
    addition.
ADD 1 cup chopped walnuts.
BLEND well.
GREASE 2 9-inch layer pans or 1
    13 × 9-inch pan
BAKE at 350° for 30 minutes.
FROST with buttercream frosting.

*BUTTERCREAM FROSTING
½ cup butter or margarine
2 cups confectioner's sugar
¼ cup milk
1 teaspoon vanilla

CREAM butter or margarine with sugar
    and milk.
BLEND until smooth.
ADD more sugar or milk until smooth
    consistency is reached.
ADD vanilla. Spread on cake.
FROSTS one 9-inch layer cake.

Option: Use only ¼ cup butter or margarine and add 3 oz. softened cream cheese; blend until smooth and mix with remaining ingredients.

Biscochitos

A very special treat at Christmas—usually served with New Mexican hot chocolate. These cookies freeze well after baking.

3 cups sifted flour
1½ teaspoons baking powder
½ teaspoon salt
1 cup lard (½ lb.)
¾ cup sugar
3 teaspoons anise seed
1 egg
¼ cup brandy or white wine
¼ cup sugar
1 teaspoon cinnamon
(Mix sugar and cinnamon; dip cookies in mixture before baking.)

SIFT dry ingredients together; set aside.
CREAM lard, sugar, and anise seeds.
BEAT egg until fluffy; add to creamed mixture.
ADD flour mixture and brandy alternately.
MIX until well blended.
KNEAD slightly and pat to form a stiff dough.
ROLL dough ¼ to ½ inch thick. Cut in circle or fleur-de-lys shape.
DIP each cookie into cinnamon-sugar mixture before baking.
BAKE at 350° on ungreased baking sheets 10–12 minutes or until lightly browned.
MAKES 3–4 dozen.

Buñuelos

A fried bread served with a glaze, buñuelos resemble the popular sopaipilla. They are a very good dessert with café con leche.

3½ cups flour
1 teaspoon salt
1 teaspoon baking powder
¼ teaspoon cinnamon
1½ tablespoons sugar
¼ cup butter
2 eggs
½ cup milk
vegetable oil for frying

SIFT dry ingredients together; cut in
    butter until mixture resembles
    cornmeal.
BEAT eggs lightly; add milk.
ADD liquid mixture to dry ingredients
    and stir until a workable dough is
    formed.
KNEAD for 2 minutes or until dough is
    smooth.
HEAT oil; pinch off dough in balls the
    size of walnuts.
ROLL out very thin into circular
    shapes.
SET dough on waxed paper until all
    dough is rolled out.
FRY each circle until puffed and golden
    brown (30 seconds).
DRAIN on absorbent towels.
DIP each into glaze, coating evenly.
DRAIN on rack until dry (about 30
    minutes).

*BUÑUELO GLAZES

Brown Sugar Glaze
½ cup brown sugar
½ cup water
1 tablespoon butter
½ teaspoon cinnamon
1 tablespoon dark corn syrup

PLACE sugar and water in saucepan.
ADD butter, cinnamon, and corn
    syrup.
HEAT, stirring until mixture boils
    1–2 minutes.
COOL 1 minute and glaze buñuelos.

Anise Glaze
1 cup brown sugar
½ cup water
1 tablespoon anise seeds
1 tablespoon butter
1 tablespoon light corn syrup

COMBINE all ingredients in
    saucepan.
COOK to boiling.
COOL, strain seeds, and glaze
    buñuelos.

Natillas

3 eggs, separated
1 tablespoon sugar
3 tablespoons cornstarch
⅛ teaspoon salt
¾ cup sugar
2¼ cups milk
cinnamon
nutmeg

BEAT egg whites, gradually adding 1 tablespoon sugar. Set aside.
DISSOLVE cornstarch, salt, and ¾ cup sugar in 1 cup milk.
BEAT egg yolks thoroughly.
STIR yolks into sugar and cornstarch mixture until it resembles a paste.
ADD paste mixture to remaining milk in saucepan over low heat.
COOK, stirring constantly, until mixture thickens.
FOLD egg whites into hot custard mixture.
CHILL in custard dishes until ready to serve.
SPRINKLE with cinnamon and nutmeg.
MAKES 8 servings.

Empanadas

An empanada is a little fruit- or meat-filled pie served during the Christmas season. In some areas, empanadas are served on other religious feast days.

*DOUGH
1 pkg. active dry yeast
1 cup lukewarm water
¼ cup lard or shortening
3 cups flour
1 teaspoon salt
oil or shortening for frying
confectioner's sugar (optional)

DISSOLVE yeast in water; set aside.
CUT shortening into dry ingredients.
　　Combine all ingredients and
　　mix well.
KNEAD until dough is satiny and
　　smooth. DO NOT let rise.
ROLL dough out ¼–⅛ inch thick
　　and cut with biscuit cutter or large
　　round cookie cutter.
PLACE filling in center of dough, fold
　　dough in half, seal edge with fork
　　tines or by pinching to give ruffled
　　effect, and fry in hot fat until
　　golden brown.
SPRINKLE with confectioner's sugar, if
　　desired, when cool.
MAKES 2 dozen little pies.

*APRICOT FILLING
½ lb. dried apricots
1½ cups water
¾ cup sugar
1 teaspoon cinnamon
1 teaspoon nutmeg

PLACE dried apricots in saucepan in
　　water.
COOK over medium heat until fruit
　　becomes moist and soft; drain.
PLACE fruit in blender along with
　　sugar and spices.
BLEND well.
PLACE filling in empanada dough and
　　fry as directed at left.

*MEAT FILLING
1 lb. roast beef or boiled beef tongue,
    shredded
1 cup raisins
⅓ cup brown sugar
⅓ cup sugar
1 teaspoon cloves
1 teaspoon cinnamon
1 cup piñon nuts or walnuts

BOIL meat immersed in water over
    medium heat in saucepan until
    tender. Drain.
TEAR meat into bite-size portions after
    cooling.
MIX meat with raisins, sugars, spices,
    and nuts.
PLACE fruit filling in empanada
    dough and fry as directed at left.

*PUMPKIN FILLING
2 cups cooked pumpkin, mashed
1 cup sugar
1 teaspoon cinnamon
1 teaspoon nutmeg
½ teaspoon cloves
½ teaspoon ginger
¼ teaspoon mace (optional)

IF using fresh pumpkin, slice, peel,
    and remove seeds; boil over
    medium heat until tender; blend
    with all other ingredients; add ¼
    to ½ cup sugar.
MIX all ingredients thoroughly.
PLACE pumpkin mixture in empanada
    dough and fry as directed at left.

Pastelitos

LITTLE PIES

*PASTRY
3 cups flour
½ teaspoon baking powder
¾ teaspoon salt
⅔ cup shortening
ice cold water (½ to ¾ cup)

*FRUIT FILLING
½ lb. dried fruit
1½ cups water
¾ cup sugar

*CINNAMON/SUGAR MIXTURE
¼ cup sugar
1 teaspoon cinnamon

PLACE dry ingredients in bowl; cut in shortening.
SPRINKLE *ice cold* water over flour.
WORK with fork to form a solid dough; set aside.
BOIL dried fruit, water, and sugar until tender. Drain.
ROLL ½ dough in 9″ × 12″ × 2″ baking sheet; place fruit filling onto dough.
ROLL remaining dough and place on top of fruit. Slit top pastry with sharp knife every 2 inches; press seams together.
SPRINKLE with sugar and cinnamon mixture, if desired, before baking.
BAKE at 375° 25–30 minutes or until golden brown. Cut into 2″ squares.
MAKES 2–3 dozen.

Flan de Caramel

1½ cups sugar
6 eggs
3½ cups milk
1 teaspoon vanilla
nutmeg

HEAT ½ cup sugar in skillet over low heat until it caramelizes.

POUR into 6 custard cups. Cool.

BEAT eggs until foamy. Add remainder of sugar, stirring until well beaten.

SCALD milk. Cool milk and gradually add egg mixture. Stir until sugar dissolves and lumps disappear. Add vanilla.

POUR into caramel-lined cups.

PLACE saucepan of hot water on lower baking rack with custard cups above.

BAKE at 350° for 1 hour and 10 minutes.

SPRINKLE with nutmeg just before serving.

MAKES 6 servings.

Capirotada

BREAD PUDDING

This New Mexican pudding is also known as sopa.

1½ cups sugar
12–14 slices day-old bread
2 tablespoons cinnamon
½ raisins
½ cup piñon nuts or chopped
    walnuts
1 cup shredded longhorn cheese
    (optional)

OVER low heat in large skillet, melt
    sugar down to syrup; meanwhile,
    tear slices of bread into bite-size
    pieces.
PLACE bread in large casserole dish;
    sprinkle with cinnamon, raisins,
    and nuts.
WHEN sugar becomes brown syrup,
    turn burner off; add 1 cup water
    (*be careful* as this will bubble over
    quickly—stand away from it.)
WHEN water is syrup color, pour
    liquid over bread mixture until
    soaked.
SPRINKLE top with grated cheese, if
    desired.
BAKE casserole at 350° 20–25
    minutes, uncovered.
SERVE hot or cold topped with
    whipping cream.
MAKES 4–6 ½-cup servings.

Arroz Dulce

SWEET RICE PUDDING

1½ cups cooked rice
2 cups evaporated milk
½ cup sugar
1 tablespoon cinnamon
2 egg whites (optional)
1 teaspoon vanilla

COMBINE rice, milk, and sugar in large saucepan.
BRING to a boil; simmer over low heat; add cinnamon.
IF DESIRED, whip 2 egg whites and add to hot rice mixture, stirring rapidly. Add vanilla.
SERVE immediately.
MAY be served cold also.
MAKES 4–5 ½-cup servings.

Compechanas

CRISPIES

Crispies are often served as a snack or a dessert with New Mexican hot chocolate or café con leche.

2¼ cups flour
1¼ oz. pkg. dry yeast
2 tablespoons sugar
½ teaspoon salt
½ teaspoon nutmeg
¾ cup warm water
3 tablespoons shortening
1 egg
¾ cup sugar
½ cup chopped pecans
¼ cup brown sugar (firmly packed)
1 teaspoon cinnamon

COMBINE 2 cups flour, yeast, 2 tablespoons sugar, salt, and nutmeg; add water, shortening and egg.

BLEND until moistened; beat 3 minutes; stir in remainder of flour to form a stiff batter. Cover; let rise 45 minutes. Stir down batter; add enough flour so dough is solid; combine ¾ cup sugar, pecans, brown sugar, and cinnamon in separate dish.

ROLL dough into 4–5-inch circles, ⅛ inch thick.

DIP circles on both sides into sugar mixture; place on well-greased cookie sheets. Bake at 400° 12–15 minutes or until golden brown; do not burn. Cool on wire rack.

MAKES 12–15 large cookies.

New Mexican Bolitas

These cookies, also known as sandies or teacakes, are found typically at weddings and other fiestas.

1 cup butter or margarine, softened	CREAM butter, sugar, and extracts.
½ cup confectioner's sugar or granulated sugar	BLEND in flour, salt, and nuts.
1 teaspoon vanilla extract	MIX until dough holds together.
1 teaspoon almond extract	FORM into 1-inch balls.
2 cups flour	BAKE on ungreased baking sheets 1 inch apart at 400° for 10–12 minutes or until lightly browned.
¼ teaspoon salt	
1 cup finely chopped pecans or walnuts	COOL a few minutes; roll in confectioner's sugar several times until well coated.
confectioner's sugar	MAKES 4 dozen small cookies.

Pan de Huevo

EGG SWEETBREAD

1 cup milk
1¼ cups sugar
2 teaspoons salt
⅔ cup shortening
6 eggs
3 ¼ oz. pkgs. dry yeast
4½ cups flour

HEAT milk until scalded; cool.
CREAM sugar, salt, and shortening, and
　　add eggs, one at a time.
ADD yeast to warm milk; add flour
　　until stiff dough is formed.
KNEAD 5–10 minutes; let dough rise
　　1 hour.
PUNCH down; form round, egg-size
　　balls; place in 2 greased 9-inch
　　round pans; cover and let rise 45
　　minutes.
PREPARE glaze paste.

*GLAZE PASTE
2 cups flour
1½ cups sugar
6 egg yolks
1 teaspoon salt
1 cup shortening
1 teaspoon vanilla extract or
　　lemon extract

MIX all ingredients well; paste should
　　be smooth.
SPREAD paste thoroughly over each
　　roll.
BAKE at 375° 25 to 30 minutes or until
　　light to golden brown.
MAKES 3–4 dozen.

Molletes

ANISE COFFEE ROLLS

1 pkg. dry yeast
1 tablespoon sugar
1 cup warm water
½ cup margarine or shortening
¾ cup sugar
2 eggs
1 teaspoon salt
2 teaspoons anise seeds
3½ cups flour

DISSOLVE yeast and 1 tablespoon sugar in warm water; cream shortening or margarine and sugar.
ADD eggs, salt, and anise seeds; blend with yeast mixture; add flour until dough is stiff.
KNEAD until dough is smooth.
LET rise 1 hour; punch dough down; shape into round rolls; place in 2 greased 9-inch round pans. Let rise 45 minutes.
BAKE at 375° 25–30 minutes.
WHILE warm, drizzle with confectioner's glaze (½ cup confectioner's sugar, 2 tablespoons water).
MAKES 1–1½ dozen.

Native Feast Cookies

These cookies resemble biscochitos, but they are a bit larger.

1½ cups sugar
1 cup shortening
¼ cup white wine or fruit brandy
1 egg
1 teaspoon vanilla
2 cups all-purpose flour
½ cup whole wheat flour
1 teaspoon baking powder
¼ teaspoon salt
½ cup chopped nuts (or piñons)

CREAM sugar and shortening.
MIX wine, egg, and vanilla.
SIFT flours, baking powder, and salt; alternate dry ingredients and liquids into creamed mixture; add nuts and mix well.
ROLL dough out on lightly floured surface. Cut in 2-inch squares.
MAKE cuts in squares in fleur-de-lys patterns.
BAKE on ungreased cookie sheet at 350° 10–12 minutes.
MAKES 2–3 dozen cookies.

Zucchini Nut Bread

2 cups raw zucchini, peeled and grated
2 cups sugar
3 eggs
1¼ cups oil
1 cup chopped nuts
3 cups flour
1 teaspoon baking powder
1 teaspoon cinnamon
½ teaspoon salt
1 teaspoon nutmeg

COMBINE zucchini, sugar, eggs, oil, and nuts.
SIFT dry ingredients.
GRADUALLY add dry ingredients to creamed mixture; mix thoroughly.
POUR into 2 well-greased loaf pans. Bake for 1 hour at 375°.
MAKES 2 loaves.

NOTE: At high altitudes (5,000 feet or more) you may want to add 2 tablespoons flour.

MISCELLANEOUS

Dried Fruits and Vegetables

Reconstitute any of these dried fruits or vegetables with water. The fruits become delicious for pies, and the vegetables are excellent in stews and soups.

*Apricots, cherries, peaches, pears, grapes, bananas, or apples
FRUIT should be at its peak (not overripe, not underripe).
HALVE apricots, cherries, and grapes.
SLICE peaches, pears, apples, and bananas ¼–½ inch thick.

*Zucchini, eggplant, or tomatoes
SLICE vegetables to ¼–½ inch thick.

PLACE halves or slices of fruit and/or vegetables on mesh trays outdoors where direct sunlight will hit trays. Keep vegetables and fruits on separate trays.
COVER with cheesecloth to prevent insects from getting on fruits and vegetables.
LEAVE in sunlight 2–3 days, rotating every several hours. Do not leave out overnight, or if weather cools down, or if there is any moisture in the air.

FRUIT or VEGETABLES should be completely dry, with no soft or moist areas. When dry, store in airtight jars or cans in cool dark area.
RECONSTITUTE with water for cooking (eat in dry form as a snack).
FRUITS may be stewed in 2 cups water, 1 cup sugar, and 2 tablespoons cornstarch for 45 minutes for use in pies.
VEGETABLES can be added to soups and stews the last 20 minutes of cooking.

NOTE: Onion stems and celery leaves may be dried in this fashion and when completely dry may be placed in blender with a little salt for onion or celery salt, if desired.

You can dry fruits and vegetables in a solar greenhouse. Leave in greenhouse 1–2 days.

Melon, Pumpkin, and Sunflower Seeds

A natural and nutritious snack for the whole family.

USE ANY OF THE FOLLOWING:

melon seeds
pumpkin seeds
sunflower seeds
salt (to taste)

WASH seeds and drain on paper towels.

PLACE seeds, salt, and water to cover in a container.

LET stand 15 minutes. For very salty taste, leave longer.

DRAIN seeds. Place on absorbent towel until all moisture is removed.

PLACE on cookie sheets in single layer.

ROAST at 325° for 25–30 minutes.

STIR seeds frequently to prevent scorching.

COOL seeds before storing.

STORE in an airtight container, out of sunlight.

Piñon Nuts

PINE NUTS

Piñon nuts (pignolia in Italian) ripen in late summer or early fall.

PLACE piñons on a cookie sheet in a single layer.
ROAST at 325° for approximately 15 minutes.
STIR piñons frequently to prevent burning.
CRACK outer shell to sample for doneness.

COOL when roasted and seal in an airtight container. Keeps up to 6 months. Freeze, if desired, to extend freshness. Thaw when ready to use; it is not necessary to cook again.

Green Chile Jelly

Why not! Good as a relish or on toast.

4 fresh green chiles
2 green bell peppers
2 teaspoons vinegar
1 cup water
4 cups sugar
1 box Sure-jell or pectin

ROAST and peel green chile; remove stems and seeds.
PLACE chile and pepper in blender and blend very fine.
BOIL peppers in vinegar and water 1½–2 hours; add sugar and pectin and pour into jars.
PLACE in hot bath for 20–25 minutes until lids seal on jars.
COOL and store in cool dark area.
MAKES 4–6 half-pint jars.

Tomé Applebutter

Mamacita made this spicy butter out of apples from her orchard in Tomé, New Mexico.

4–6 dozen apples, peeled and cored
3 cups sugar
2 tablespoons cider vinegar
2 tablespoons cinnamon
1 teaspoon nutmeg
¼ cup butter

BOIL sliced apples until they are very tender, about 2 hours, in water to cover; replenish water as necessary.

DRAIN excess water when apples are done.

ADD sugar, vinegar, spices, and butter; mix well.

SIMMER 5–10 minutes.

PLACE in blender; blend until smooth.

PLACE in jars in hot bath and steam under pressure 15–20 minutes; make sure jar lids seal.

MAKES 8–10 pint jars.

NOTE: This is very good on toast or tortillas.

Trini's Pear Leather

2½ lbs. pears
½ cup sugar
1 teaspoon lemon juice

PEEL ripe pears.
SLICE pears to measure one quart;
    then mash. Transfer to saucepan.
ADD sugar and lemon juice.
HEAT slowly until juices form.
SIMMER 15–20 minutes.
STIR frequently until slightly
    thickened. Cool.
BLEND in a blender to smooth
    consistency.
COVER cookie sheet with freezer wrap
    or waxed paper.
SPREAD pulp ¼ inch thick on
    covered cookie sheet.
COVER with cheesecloth and place in
    the sun 8–10 hours.
REPEAT this process for three days or
    until leather is no longer sticky.
REMOVE from paper, cut in strips,
    and roll.
SEAL in airtight container.

NOTE: Pear leather may also be dried
in a food dehydrator, convection oven,
or very low oven (approximately
10–12 hours).

Index